Democracy and welfare ec

Democracy and welfare economics

HANS VAN DEN DOEL

PROFESSOR OF ECONOMICS, UNIVERSITY OF AMSTERDAM

TRANSLATED BY BRIGID BIGGINS

CAMBRIDGE UNIVERSITY PRESS

CAMBRIDGE

LONDON · NEW YORK · MELBOURNE

Published by the Syndics of the Cambridge University Press
The Pitt Building, Trumpington Street, Cambridge CB2 1RP
Bentley House, 200 Euston Road, London NW1 2DB
32 East 57th Street, New York, NY 10022, USA
296 Beaconsfield Parade, Middle Park, Melbourne 3206, Australia

English translation first published 1979
This work was originally published in Dutch in 1975 (2nd edn 1978)
by Samson Uitgeverij, Alphen aan den Rijn under the title
Demokratie en welvaartstheorie

Phototypeset by
Western Printing Services Ltd, Bristol
Printed in Great Britain at the
University Press, Cambridge

Library of Congress Cataloguing in Publication Data
Doel, Hans van den.
Democracy and welfare economics.
Translation of Demokratie en welvaartstheorie.
Bibliography: p. 154
Includes indexes.
1. Welfare economics. 2. Democracy.
3. Bureaucracy. I. Title.
HB99.3.D6313   330.15′5   78–21660
ISBN 0 521 22568 X hard covers
ISBN 0 521 29555 6 paperback

Contents

Preface   ix
Acknowledgements   xi

1 Democracy and bureaucracy   1

  1.1 Economics and politics   1
    Centralisation and government   1
    Some shortcomings of economics and political science 2
    Economic theory of political decision-making   5
    Methodological individualism   6
    Welfare economics   7

  1.2 Democracy and bureaucracy   9
    Economic power and economic order   9
    The concepts of 'democracy' and 'bureaucracy'   10
    The development of the concept of democracy   11
    The development of the concept of bureaucracy   13
    The political system   14

2 The welfare optimum   18

  2.1 Rationality   18
    Aim   18
    Consistency   20
    Maximisation   21
    Measuring utility   23

  2.2 Optimum utility   25
    Indivisibility   25
    Exclusion by producers   26
    External effects   27
    Exclusion of the consumer   28
    Optimum utility   30

  2.3 Optimum economic welfare   32
    The demand for a social good   32
    The interpersonal comparison of utility   33
    Economic welfare function   35
    The Pareto criterion   36
    The economic welfare optimum   38

3 Negotiation 41

3.1 Negotiations democracy 41
Freedom of exit and non-commitment 41
Self-interest and 'class interest' 42
Exchange 44
The Prisoners' Dilemma 47

3.2 Negotiations democracy and economic welfare 50
Political participation and economic welfare 50
Collective action and economic welfare 53
The democratic acceptance of coercion 56
Economic welfare without coercion? 58
The end of 'laissez-faire' 61

3.3 Negotiations democracy in practice 62
Defence and development cooperation 62
Full employment and the social contract 64
A discussion on the 'democratic acceptance of coercion' 68

4 Majority decision 73

4.1 Majority and utility 73
The economic policy optimum theorem 73
A simple or a qualified majority? 75
The iron law of oligarchy 77

4.2 Majority and rationality 78
The macro-political paradox 78
Extremism and democracy 80
The fiscal debate: an empirical example 82

4.3 Majority and economic welfare 85
Passionate minorities 85
Logrolling: an example 87
Alternative voting systems 90

5 Representation 94

5.1 The demand for government policy 94
Elected representatives 94
The influence of income 95
The concepts of 'left' and 'right' 97
Indifference and alienation 99
Empirical data 100

5.2 The supply of government policy 103
The aims of politicians 103
The dynamics of political parties 104
Inconsistency and unreliability 106
Policy polarisation 107

Some empirical evidence 109
The assumptions of the model 110

5.3 Democracy and economic welfare 113
Democracy and the Pareto criterion 113
Democracy and the neo-Paretian criterion 115
Political competition 117
Political information 118

6 Implementation 121

6.1 The power of bureaucracy 121
Bilateral monopoly 121
The limitation of a bureaucracy 122
The *homo economicus sovieticus* 124
The aims of a bureaucrat 125

6.2 Bureaucratic behaviour 127
Niskanen's model 127
The bureaucratic optimum 129
The compromise between parliament and the administration 131
A note on empirical investigations 131

6.3 Bureaucracy and economic welfare 132
Contraction or expansion? 132
Private firms 134
Self-management by civil servants 137

7 The political process 144

7.1 The political process as a number of production stages 144
7.2 The welfare effects of the four decision-making models 145
7.3 The public sector: a huge Leviathan? 149

Bibliography 154
Index of subjects 164
Index of names 171

Preface

This book is the English edition of *Demokratie en welvaartstheorie*, which was first published in the Netherlands in 1975. It soon became required reading at four Dutch universities for graduate students in welfare economics, economic policy, public finance or public administration. This English edition is based on the second Dutch edition (1978).

Democracy and welfare economics is an attempt to integrate economics and political science, as applied to the democratic method of decision-making. My aims in publishing this book are educational, scientific and political.

The educational aim is to revivify teaching in welfare economics, economic policy, public finance, and political science to non-mathematical students, by bringing them into contact with a new area of applied welfare economics which has great social significance, thus stimulating their interest in welfare economics.

The scientific aim is to deepen the insight into the welfare effects of the democratic method of decision-making in the public sector. I shall attempt to achieve this aim in two ways. First, by bringing together and integrating the relevant economic theories of decision-making, which are not only spread widely over may different publications but also apply to a wide variety of subjects. Integration is achieved by means of the concept of a 'political process' – here understood to mean the production stages which link the original political producer with the final political consumer. Second, contrary to custom, welfare economics is not regarded as a normative theory (which lays down how a society should be arranged) but as a positive theory, which links the actual organisation of society and the consequent level of satisfaction among the individuals of that society.

The political aim is to make clear when, and under what conditions, it is socially efficient to apply democratic decision-making in solving economic problems (such as unemployment, inflation, social insecurity, environmental pollution, and inner city decay). During the six and a half years (1967–73) I was a member of the Labour Party in the Dutch Parliament, I experienced almost daily how the solution of economic problems was made more difficult because economists saw political democracy as a disruptive element in economic policy, while politicians felt that certain democratic decision-making models were sacrosanct. I hope to strengthen democracy and to stimulate the extended use of democratic decision-making by giving suggestions, based on scientific analysis, about a 'democratic acceptance of coercion' when fixing wages and other incomes, preventing a tyranny of the majority, ensuring a control of the voter over cabinet policies, and eliminating government bureaucracy as a basis for power.

For maximum benefit the reader must bear the following in mind. This is not a book about unemployment, inflation or incomes policy – it is concerned with democracy. The social problems discussed serve primarily as case-histories and must be considered from one aspect only, viz. economic decision-making. A vast number of economic and political factors have been ignored, such as inequalities of income and technological development. Had I also taken these facets into account, I might have reached other conclusions. This, too, is why no absolute validity may be attributed to the conclusions reached in this book.

Amsterdam, 1 May 1978.   H.V.D.D.

Acknowledgements

This book has its source in the 'theory of the optimum regime' of my mentor and friend Jan Tinbergen. He also encouraged me to complete it and to let it be published not only in my native Dutch but also in English.

Piet Hennipman, my predecessor in the chair of welfare economics and economic policy, contributed most generously from his wide knowledge of welfare economics and of methodology by reading the manuscript twice and by making comments, some of which touched on very fundamental matters. His original approach to problems and the charming manner in which he saved me from error, did much to improve this book.

My wife, Truus Grondsma, made vital contributions to this book. In addition to reading most of the literature on the subject, she also planned the design and content of many sections and critically examined the resulting work both as a whole and in its (mathematical) detail.

Many colleagues provided help. I single out for especial thanks: Michael Ellman, Joop Klant, Reinier Krooshof and Arend Vermaat who took the trouble to read the book critically. Their criticisms forced me to seek to be more precise.

Finally, Brigid Biggins translated with much patience, care and skill.

All these persons deserve – and are given – my deep and lasting appreciation.

H.V.D.D.

I

Democracy and bureaucracy

1.1 Economics and politics

Centralisation and government

One of the most radical changes which has occurred in the Atlantic economies during the past three quarters of this century has been the rapid growth of the public sector. Pryor (1973, p. 14) mentions that in the USA and Canada already in 1955 about 23 per cent of the measurable national capital (the supply of dwellings excluded) was concentrated in the public sector. This percentage was even higher in the United Kingdom. In Britain at the present time, the electricity, gas, railways, aircraft, coal, shipbuilding, and (bulk) steel industries are wholly in the public sector. In addition, major parts of the broadcasting, air transport, road transport, nuclear, motor vehicle, and oil industries are also in the public sector. Furthermore, a large part of the housing stock is publicly owned.

Centralisation of power by the government took place not only through the growth of public ownership but also by the introduction of statutory control of various aspects of business policy: wages, prices, social security, safety, competition, the environment, and town and country planning. Many aspects of decisions taken by private firms regarding production and prices are subject to such legal requirements.

However, the most radical centralisation of economic power did not come about by either ownership or statutory measures, but by a relative increase in the production of social and quasi-social goods. Table 1.1 gives some data collected by the OECD on ten Western, mainly Atlantic, economies.

In 1974 current expenditure on goods and services of the general governments amounted to 15 to 20 per cent of the gross domestic product (GDP), whereas current transfer payments were 9 to 26 per cent of GDP. Total government expenditure, which in most countries in 1890 had totalled less than 10 per cent of gross national

TABLE 1.1 *Income and expenditure of the general government in ten countries in 1974* (as a percentage of GDP)

Country	current expenditure on goods and services	current transfer payments	current revenue
Australia	15.4	9.1	28.9
Canada	19.2	11.7	38.6
Denmark	23.2	15.8	47.4
France	13.0	20.8	38.9
Germany	19.7	16.6	41.4
Netherlands	17.2	26.6	51.4
Norway	16.5	22.4	48.5
Sweden	23.6	18.7	49.4
United Kingdom	20.5	14.8	40.0
United States	18.8	9.9	30.2

Source: OECD Economic Surveys

product at factor cost, had risen to 30 to 45 per cent of GNP in 1974. Figure 1.1 shows the rise for three countries. In the same period, the total incidence of taxation and social insurance contributions rose in the ten countries given in Table 1.1 from 29 to 51 per cent of GDP. This means that in these countries between one third and one half of national income is spent, one way or another, via the public sector.

Some shortcomings of economics and political science

The growth of the public sector has posed serious problems for economics and political science. I shall begin with economics. Robbins (1935, p. 16) defined economics as 'the science which studies human behaviour as a relationship between ends and scarce means which have alternative uses'. This definition gives no specific economic ends: each end has an economic aspect, provided it involves the use of scarce means, i.e. if the realisation of the end involves forgoing the other desired alternatives. Nor are there any specific economic means: each means is economic provided it is scarce and has alternative uses; a material good is an economic means, but so is the vote which the voter can give to one political party once every four years.

Thus economists (in the tradition of Robbins) view human behaviour from the viewpoint of scarcity. They examine what benefits and costs are involved in certain decisions. When the supply of goods and services is not limitless, people are forced to make a choice: a choice to achieve (to some extent) one end means that the achievement (to some extent) of another end must be forgone. Every choice demands sacrifices consisting of the benefits of the forgone goods and services: 'You can't have your cake and eat it.'

Figure 1.1 *Public expenditure as a percentage of GNP*

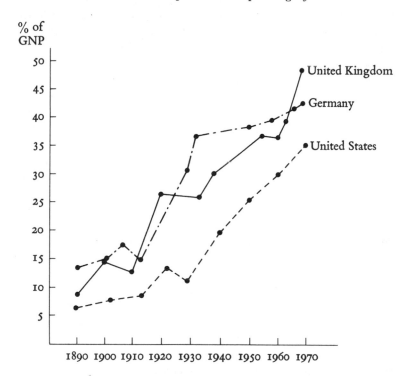

Source: Musgrave and Musgrave, 1976, p. 134. © 1976 McGraw-Hill Book Company. Used with permission of McGraw-Hill Book Company

In theory economics is an indispensable ancillary science for analysing the choices which must be made within a large public sector. In practice, however, economists ever since Adam Smith have concentrated on the private sector of the economy. The study of the public sector has been left largely to sociologists, and more recently, to political scientists. Insofar as economists have included the government in their analysis, they have generally applied the following limitations to themselves. Firstly, they have tended to regard the government, using a monistic concept, as a unitary being, i.e. as an independent individual which maximises its own utility and makes its own cost–benefit analyses. This assumption has been made explicit by Wagner (1883), Walras (1896) and Pigou (1920). Secondly, they have usually spoken of the government in normative terms only. Their main subject of discussion has been what the government should do or should refrain from doing. What the government in fact did was merely important because it enabled economists to determine to what extent the norms were met. If, contrary to expectations, the government satisfied the standards, they were pleasantly surprised or saw it as proof of their own powers of persuasion in public discussion. When the standards were unfortunately not met by the government they took offence, felt despondent or they called for the present politicians to be replaced by better ones. Only Pareto (1906) among his contemporaries drew the one correct conclusion when he said that he wanted to study sociology in order to discover why the advice of economists was ignored.

Despite the undoubted value of sociological studies, especially political science or policy sciences, they, too, have not yet succeeded in providing an adequate insight into the workings of the public sector – something which their practitioners readily admit (Mitchell, 1967; Waldo, 1972; Ostrom, 1973). David Easton defines political science as: 'those interactions by which values authoritatively are allocated for a society' (Easton, 1965b, p. 21). This can best be paraphrased as political science investigating how society allots its values (goods, services, etc.) which *bind* individuals (Easton, 1965a, p. 50). I do not wish to enter into the discussion among political scientists on when an allocation of values is binding. It is important to note, however, that most political scientists assume that it is precisely the institutions of the public sector (pressure groups, political parties, parliament, cabinet, civil servants) that bring about this binding allocation. Thus, not only economics but also political science is an important, even essential, ancillary science for studying the theory of the public sector.

But in practice political scientists do not justify this claim. Political scientists who work from Easton's definition generally neglect the economic aspect of the allocation of values. For the purposes of this book it is important that many political scientists ignore the fact that the institutions of the public sector have costs as well as benefits. Here costs do not mean the costs of salaries and housing of the office and its staff, but are related to the fact that these institutions do not always decide on an optimum allocation of values (goods and services) which are relatively scarce. The chance that the decisions will be wrong ones as regards the citizens is considerably greater if the process of choosing is wrongly organised. Thus, binding allocations of values by public sector institutions is not only a sociological but also an economic problem. It is only when political scientists realise the validity of this conclusion that the results of their analyses will be satisfactory.

Economic theory of political decision-making

The shortcomings in the way in which most economists and political scientists study the public sector can be reduced when economics, sociology and political science are integrated into a new field. A beginning was made with such an integration when, after the Second World War, a new field of economics and political science was developed in the writings of Arrow, Baumol, Downs, Musgrave, Olson, Buchanan, Tullock, Riker and Niskanen and which was given many names (*'theory of public choice'*, Buchanan and Tollison, 1972; *'mathematical political theory'*, Taylor, 1971; *'the study of non-market decisionmaking'*, Mueller, 1976), two of which describe this new field best (Frey, 1970a, p. 1), viz.: *'the economic theory of political decision-making'* and *'the new political economy'*.

This field is *new* because a large-scale use is made of deductive methods of analysis and of mathematical models. A mathematical model is a system of mathematical equations which fit together logically. A combination of deductive theorising and mathematical formulation may provide a number of advantages; the implications of certain assumptions are less easily overlooked; contradictions in logic in the assumptions can be clarified; whoever formulates a theory is forced to list exactly to which phenomena the elements of his theory will apply; complicated structures can sometimes be described more easily; and, last but not least, it becomes easier to test some points of political theories quantitatively. Frey (1970a, p. 21) concludes rightly that such a confrontation with reality, which he terms politometrics, can prevent the building of mathematical models from becoming the end rather than the means.

The new field is part of *political science* because it is concerned with *positive* theories which consider binding decisions made by society about the allocation of values. Special attention is paid to the way in which *government policy* is made. Until now the most important themes of the economic theory of political decision-making have been: supply and demand of social goods within a group, the alloca-

tion of values in the process of exchange with different power
constellations, the influence on government policy of competition
among political parties for votes, and the behaviour of bureaucratic
organisations.

Finally, the new field is also part of *economics*, both as regards the
object of study and the method used. I have already noted that
economics, as defined by Robbins, studies the decisions taken with
respect to relatively scarce goods and services. Thus the economic
theory of political decision-making studies the decisions taken with
respect to relatively scarce *social and quasi-social goods*. The theory is
especially concerned with how the allocation of these scarce goods is
influenced by the *method of decision-making*. Peter Wiles (1962, p. 1)
inadvertently formulates the basis of the economic theory of political
decision-making when he assumes '*that there is such a thing as the logic
of institutions: that an economic model will function in the way that it does,
and have the political effects it has, partly for internal, purely economic
reasons inaccessible to the sociologist or historian*'.

Methodological individualism

In respect of *method*, Klaver and Siccama (1974, p. 128) speak of a
'structural isomorphism' (i.e. a similarity of form) between the
economic theory of political decision-making on the one hand, and
micro-economics on the other. This is apparent from the use of the
deductive method (discussed above), from the assumption that decisions taken by individuals in an economy are intended to maximise
the attainment of some objective (see pp. 18–23), from the postulate
of '*methodological individualism*'. The monistic concept of the government as an unitary ('superhuman') economic subject is replaced
by a pluralistic concept in which the government is seen as a set of
individuals (the suppliers) who produce social goods for a set of
other individuals (the buyers) who value these social goods on their
individual merits.

On the *supply side*, methodological individualism provides a much
more thorough insight into decision-making within the government. The government is not seen as a mythical institution raised
high above the citizens, but as a set of groups (pressure groups,
politicians, civil servants) and individuals (the trade unionist, the
politician of party X, the civil servant of department Y) who may all
be pursuing aims which conflict in parts. This view does not permit
an 'own responsibility' of *the* government (e.g. for the taking of
paternalistic decisions) although it allows extraordinary positions

of power for particular individuals who can in consequence take paternalistic decisions on *their* own account and experience the political consequences.

On the *demand side*, methodological individualism was introduced by Sax, Mazzola and Wicksell many years ago to the theory of public finance; it has become highly relevant because of the growth of the public sector. As far back as 1935, when the public sector was half its present size, Mannheim warned about the growing power of the 'state' over 'society'. This warning is being taken more and more seriously. When collective decisions are taken about what is a large part of everyone's income, many have serious questions about the status of the individual. Some of these questions are: whose aims determine collective decisions, what decisions are taken, and how are the costs and benefits of these decisions allocated among the citizens? The increasing size and complexity of the public sector make it wellnigh impossible for voters to know what is important for the benefit of other voters. Even in 1896 Wicksell concluded that *'each person can ultimately speak only for himself'*. The parcel of goods and services provided by the public sector can only be at an optimum if economic welfare, as seen by the individual citizens, is thus able to reach the highest possible level.

Welfare economics

More or less extensive surveys of economic theories on political decision-making have been given by Attali (1972), Riker and Ordeshook (1973), Frey (1978), Frohlich and Oppenheimer (1978) and Mueller (1976, 1979). Although not all of these surveys are easily accessible, I do not feel it is necessary to provide yet another survey. Partly on the basis of the economic theories of political decision-making I want to express in this book my own view, which differs from the existing views in at least three respects:
(1) The economic theories of political decision-making are applied to the organisation of democracy and of bureaucracy in modern Western economies.
(2) The relevant theories are integrated using the concept of a 'political process' which consists of a number of stages succeeding each other logically (viz. negotiation, majority decision, representation, and implementation).
(3) The decision-making at each stage of this process is evaluated using welfare economics.
The concepts of democracy, bureaucracy and political process will

be discussed in the second half of this Chapter (1.2) so that I can confine my attention here to the role welfare economics plays in this book.

Welfare economists concentrate on *economic welfare*, which is not the group's material wealth but the group's *well-being* insofar as it depends on economic factors. Welfare economics consists of three elements:

(1) The formulation of the conditions which must be met if the economic welfare of the individuals in a group is to be at an optimum.

(2) The study of how these conditions can be *realised* by the institutions of this group and by means of policies which will be carried out within the framework of these institutions.

(3) The critical assessment of the contribution of *existing* group institutions and the existing group policy to economic welfare.

This definition means that it is precisely welfare economics which has most in common with political science. After all, both political science and welfare economics study the allocation of values for a group, in this case, for society. However, welfare economics is not concerned with society's allocation of values alone, but with the resulting social benefits and the social costs. When, in this book, I concentrate on the welfare aspects of a single allocation, I choose *ipso facto* a one-sided approach. Welfare economics, like economics in general, is a science that deals with only one aspect of reality; it studies the phenomena it observes from only one aspect, viz. the aspect of scarcity. Society's allocation of values which are not scarce falls outside its scope.

Pareto, Barone, Lange, Tinbergen and Baumol have concentrated on the welfare economic problem of defining the conditions for realising an optimum economic welfare and on the question of how the organisation of an economy (the economic order) affects the economic welfare of the totality of individuals. Tinbergen (1959, 1967), especially, makes this problem explicit when he sketches the 'optimum regime'. His question is: What economic order ensures the greatest welfare benefits, i.e. which economic order transforms individual preferences into an allocation of scarce means in such a way that economic welfare most closely approaches the optimum? This question will also form one of the mainstays of this book. Whereas Tinbergen concentrates his inquiry on the welfare aspects of the organisation of the economy as a whole, this book will consider the effects of the organisation of the *public sector* on economic welfare. I have stylised my problem in a block diagram (Figure 1.2).

Figure 1.2 *The problem of economic welfare examined in this book*

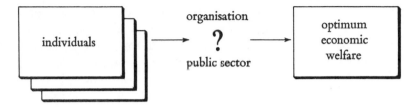

1.2 Democracy and bureaucracy

Economic power and economic order

My interest in the public sector is thus concentrated on its most fundamental element: its organisation. An economic organisation has at least three important features:

(1) It is directed at, or helps determine, the realisation of a complex of aims external to that of the organisation.
(2) It has a structure characterised by the degree of centralisation and concentration of economic power.
(3) It has a method of coordinating economic decisions related to this structure.

Ellemers (1969, p. 11), following Max Weber, defines power as a specific form of influence, viz. that influence which is backed by negative sanctions. Combining this with Robbins' definition of economics suggests that *the economic power of an agency – or a person – is its influence insofar as it can be used in accordance with its aims and is backed by the capacity to apply negative economic sanctions.* At p. 57 an example will be given of a negative economic sanction.

As already noted the structure of an economic order is characterised above all by the degree of centralisation and concentration of economic power. A structure is centralised or concentrated if the power is limited to a relatively small number of agencies or persons. In a deconcentrated or decentralised economy, power is divided equally between the agencies or persons concerned. The difference between deconcentration and decentralisation lies in the direction in which power is consolidated or spread. Concentration and deconcentration are *horizontal* movements, i.e. consolidation or separation of agencies on the same hierarchical level. Centralisation and decentralisation are *vertical* movements, i.e. consolidation of agencies on a higher hierarchical level and the separation of agencies at a lower hierarchical level respectively.

The coordination of the decisions in an organisation is largely a matter of communication. A specific pattern of lines of communication belongs to a certain structure. Bound up with the structural patterns described above there are, in principle, two patterns of communication, viz. one consisting of horizontal and one consisting of vertical relations. Horizontal relations are connections between agencies or persons on the same hierarchical level, vertical relations are relations between agencies and persons of different hierarchical levels. In other words, horizontal relations are based on *equality* of power of the agencies and persons, vertical relations are based on *inequality* of power.

Whether horizontal or vertical relations will dominate thus depends on the structure. A centralised structure means that vertical relations between the agencies and persons will dominate, a deconcentrated structure means the domination of horizontal relations.

The concepts of 'democracy' and 'bureaucracy'

I have already described the organisation of the economy as the *economic order*. Translated into the terminology just given, the economic order is, on the one hand, the degree of centralisation and concentration of the economic power of decision-making in an economy and, on the other, the related way in which the decisions are coordinated. It is noteworthy that the theory of the economic order also makes use of typologies which are based on a division into horizontal and vertical forms of coordination. Following German authors such as Eucken (1940; 1959), Hayek (1944) and Röpke (1954), two ideal types of main forms of the economic order are distinguished, viz. the *'zentralgeleitete Wirtschaft'* (centrally planned economy) and the *'Verkehrswirtschaft'* (exchange economy). The *centrally planned economy* is an ideal type of vertical organisation in which the economic actions in an economy are determined by the plan of one agency or individual. An *exchange economy* is a type of horizontal organisation in which all agencies or individuals make separate plans which they coordinate by a process of exchange.

If we consider the German terminologies literally, they have a very wide meaning. A 'zentralgeleitete Wirtschaft' does not only mean the (vertical) forms of organisation in which coordination is by personal commands but also those forms in which orders are given by means of an anonymous manipulation of markets and prices. A 'Verkehrswirtschaft' includes not only the (horizontal) forms of coordination when goods are exchanged in a market *for an amount of money per unit*, but also coordination by way of negotiations, voting or elections.

This book, however, is not a treatise on the economic order as a whole, but only on one part of it, viz. the economic order *within the public sector*. A public sector is characterised by the fact that, among other things, there is no exchange of goods for money and also that such an exchange often is impossible (see Chapter 2). Nevertheless, in a public sector it is, in principle, possible to have both Eucken's ideal types, albeit in a specific form. The ideal type of the 'zentralgeleitete Wirtschaft' in the public sector has the form of a perfect *bureaucracy*. The ideal type of the 'Verkehrswirtschaft' in the public sector has the form of a perfect *democracy*. Within a perfect bureaucracy (economic) actions are determined by the plan of a single individual, the head of the bureaucracy. The other individuals have a subordinate position in the hierarchy. The channels of communication are vertical and coordination is by ways of commands (letters, budgets, etc.). Within a perfect democracy, however, all individuals make plans independently and their power is equal. The channels of communication are horizontal and coordination is by way of negotiations, unanimous decisions, simple (or qualified) majorities and/or by delegating decision-making to elected representatives. Thus, I define *bureaucracy as a collection of methods to coordinate (outside the market) the decisions of agencies which, and persons who, are subordinate to each other in the hierarchy*. On the other hand, I define *democracy as a collection of methods to coordinate (outside the market) the decisions of agencies and persons who have equal positions*.

The development of the concept of democracy

The formal definition of 'democracy' given above is but one of many. Some authors do not regard democracy as a type of organisation but as a certain condition of *economic welfare*, not as a method of production but as a product. According to Braybrooke (1968) democracy is the production of all the best: 'personal rights, human welfare, collective preference'. This is also the Marxist–Leninist conception of democracy.

Other authors view democracy as a certain attitude of the voters, e.g. a tolerant attitude to the opinions of others, or the desire to reach a certain degree of consensus (e.g. the article on democracy in the *Handwörterbuch der Sozialwissenschaften* begins: 'Democracy . . . is less a type of government than a way of life'). Chapter 4 examines this aspect of democracy more closely (pp. 80–2).

Yet others regard democracy as a type of organisation, but as having a certain structure (Dahl, 1956, pp. 34–5). According to Madison, who before he became President of the USA had exerted great influence on the American constitution, democracy is the same as deconcentration. He saw the essence of democracy as the protection of minorities against majorities, and of majorities against minorities; he felt that this protection should be provided by 'external checks' which lay not in periodic elections but in the horizontal spread over a number of institutions, e.g. the legislative and executive power. On the other hand, the present adherents of 'basic democracy' consider that democracy is the same as *decentralisation*. They advocate a spread of the power to take decisions over the 'political base', which means a decentralisation so that everyone is master in his own house.

The concept of democracy as a formal method of coordinating the decisions of agencies and persons with equal positions goes back to the Greeks, who introduced the concept of democracy as a type of political organisation, viz. that type in which the definitive decisions of the *polis* (city state) were taken by a majority of votes in the assembly in which all members were equal. Aristotle, for example, concluded that democracy is indeed based on equality, but that one can only speak of it when 'the people are in the majority and what they vote is law'. Since then numerous writers have associated democracy with the rule of the majority. According to Locke a democratic community has 'one body, with a power to act as one body, which is only by the will and determination of the majority'. Rousseau considered that unanimity was necessary for decisions on the *contrat social* but 'apart from this . . . contract, the vote of the majority always binds all the rest'. President Jefferson said in his first inaugural address: 'The first principle of republicanism is that the *lex majoris partis* (the majority rule) is the fundamental law of every society of individuals of equal votes.' A later president, Lincoln, went even further in his first inaugural address when he said that if the majority principle is rejected 'anarchy or despotism in some form is all that is left'. De Tocqueville, too, concludes: 'The very essence of democratic government consists in the absolute sovereignty of the majority' (Dahl, 1956, pp. 34–5).

In their definitions Jefferson, Lincoln and De Tocqueville, all of whom lived in the nineteenth century, stressed only one method of decision-making in a democracy, the majority decision. By then representative democracy had already been analysed systematically by, among others, De Tocqueville (1835; 1948) and John Stuart Mill (*Considerations on Representative Government*, 1861) but it had not been regarded as an essential part of democracy. This was not done until Schumpeter. The publication of his book *Capitalism, Socialism and Democracy* (1943) was an important step forward because he considered democracy as a type of horizontal coordination which is comparable to the market mechanism. His definition is: 'The democratic method is that institutional arrangement for arriving at political decisions in which individuals acquire the power to decide by means of a competitive struggle for the people's vote' (Schumpeter, 1954, p. 269). This definition made Schumpeter the forerunner of the new political economics. My own definition in which all horizontal methods of coordination (which operate outside the market) are considered a part of democracy has a more general application, though, and is thus more suited to the purposes of this book.

The development of the concept of bureaucracy

Not only is my definition of 'democracy' specific, so also is my definition of 'bureaucracy'. In Albrow's survey (1970) of changes in the concept of bureaucracy it is apparent that some writers do not regard bureaucracy as a special type of organisation but as an organisation with a certain positive or negative *result*. Weber (1922; 1964) defines bureaucracy as that 'organisation that maximises efficiency in management' whereas Crozier (1964, p. 187) defines bureaucracy as 'an organisation that cannot correct its behaviour by learning from its errors'. In the first view bureaucracy is a rational organisation, in the second it is irrational.

Those authors who do regard bureaucracy as a type of organisation have also been greatly influenced by Weber. He described bureaucracy as a management apparatus which is specified by an explicit bureaucratic hierarchy in which bureaucrats are employees with a labour contract, follow a fixed career pattern, and are subject to disciplinary measures. Two concepts are discernible in the post-Weberian literature, viz. the external and the internal view of democracy; both views are based on Weber's ideas.

The *external* view means that bureaucracy is seen as a type of society in which bureaucrats manage the whole or part of society.

This view has been elaborated mainly by macro-sociologists such as Parsons and Etzioni but it is also shared by some economists, for example, John Stuart Mill (1861) and by Von Mises who, in his monograph *Bureaucracy* (1945), fought against the bureaucratisation of society as it would mean the downfall of a private enterprise motivated by the desire for profit.

Although Weber shared the external view of bureaucracy he described the inner workings of a bureaucratic system in such detail that he also laid the foundations of the *internal* view which sees bureaucracy as a certain type of internal organisation (of a department, or a political party, or a firm). Organisation sociologists such as Simon (1957; 1965), Blau (1963) and Scott have elaborated this view.

Weber analyses bureaucracy in the public sector only. Michels (1911; 1962) noted that a bureaucratic hierarchy does not occur solely in government but also in private organisations such as clubs and firms. According to him a hierarchy is essential within an organisation. The best-known economist, who, though holding the internal view of bureaucracy does not limit it to government, is Downs. He defines bureaucracy as an organisation of which the major portion of its output is not directly or indirectly evaluated in any markets external to the organisation. He has worked out the internal organisation of such a bureaucracy in great detail in his book *Inside Bureaucracy* (1966).

My own definition of bureaucracy, in which all vertical methods to coordinate decisions taken outside the market are seen as a form of bureaucracy, is in fact based entirely on Weber's definition. It is sufficiently wide to combine the external and internal views of bureaucracy and is therefore incorporated in this book.

The political system

In Weber's terminology the concepts of 'democracy' and 'bureaucracy' are *ideal types*, i.e. abstractions containing only the pure elements from which a concrete political system is constructed. The rest of this chapter will be devoted to the concrete political system. In principle, a system is a set of elements, which can be limited in number and which are mutually related. The term 'political system' primarily acquired a meaning by Easton's writings (1965a, 1965b). In complete harmony with his definition of political science (p. 4) Easton defines a political system as 'those interactions through which values are authoritatively allocated for a society'. In respect of such a political system and its environment, three elements are usually distinguished: a *culture* (including the aims of the individuals belonging to the system), a *structure* (including the balance of power), and a *process* (by which the decisions are coordinated according to a certain method and the binding allocations of values is established).

The special feature of Easton's analysis is that he describes this *process* using an open system concept. The political system receives *inputs* from the environment. These inputs are the demands of individuals on policy and the support they give certain officials. The inputs are *converted* by the political system into *outputs*, i.e. into decisions on policy, such as the production and distribution of social goods and the laying down of rules of taxation. The policy affects the *environment* (e.g. the type of schools, the structure of cities, the distribution of income) and thus the individuals are affected. These effects, which consist of costs and benefits, in their turn influence the demands and the support of the individuals, and the cycle begins again. The political process as described by Easton is stylised simply in Figure 1.3 in a form suitable for this book.

Figure 1.3 *Flow model of a political process in an open system*

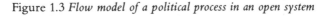

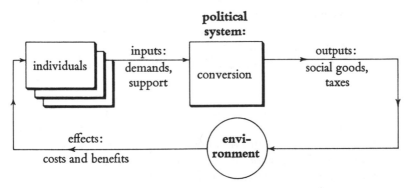

Source: Grondsma and Van den Doel, 1975, p. 201

The flow model of the political process throws light on the fact that 'parliamentary democracy' which is a feature of some twenty Western economies is a complicated process of decision-making which passes through a number of different stages. In my opinion each of these stages can be split up into a number of sub-stages. For example, the process of conversion, in which the aims of individuals are transformed into social goods and services, in its turn has four stages in each of which a different decision-making method dominates, viz. negotiation, majority decision, representation and implementation. The order in which I mention these stages and their respective methods of decision-making is not based on chronology but on logic. For example, I do not exclude the possibility that a majority decision or some kind of negotiation will follow the representation. The logic of the order is that – naturally with the exception of negotiation – none of the stages can exist unless the system has passed through the previous stage at least once. This will be illustrated in Chapter 7 (pp. 144–5).

In this book two elements of the flow model will be examined more closely: the process of conversion and the evaluation of its effects. The criteria on which this evaluation is based are considered in Chapter 2. The following chapters (3 to 6) will analyse the decision-making methods which are relevant to the four successive stages of the process of conversion, as independent decision-making models, viz.

(1) *Negotiations democracy*. This stage is examined in Chapter 3; it consists of negotiations between the agencies and persons concerned and it aims at reaching a result acceptable to the largest possible majority. An example of such a negotiations democracy is the 'concerted action' of employers, workers and representatives of the government on the division of the national income between wages, profits, and expenditure on social goods and services.

(2) *Referendum democracy*. This stage is examined in Chapter 4; it consists of the decision whether to put the results of the negotiations to the vote, in which case the outcome of the voting is binding. A referendum democracy is not confined to referendums on a single proposal, but it may also be used to vote upon a whole bunch of decisions, such as happens when general elections are held.

(3) *Representative democracy*. This stage is examined in Chapter 5; it consists of letting elected representatives conduct the negotiations and take the majority decisions. As Schumpeter has pointed out, these elected representatives compete amongst themselves for the support of the voters. Examples of such a representative democracy are the negotiations within, and the decisions by, a parliament and a cabinet.

(4) *Implementation bureaucracy*. This stage is examined in Chapter 6;

it is concerned with whether or not decisions taken by parliament and the cabinet are implemented by appointed bureaucrats. Examples of such an implementation bureaucracy are the decision-making processes within ministries and within each department of a ministry.

A political process can be compared with a branch of industry specialising in the production of social goods and services. The four stages mentioned are then production stages which link the original producer with the final consumer. In the stages of negotiations democracy and referendum democracy the raw materials can be said to be produced, the intermediate goods are then the product of the representative democracy while the implementation bureaucracy provides the final product for immediate consumption. As is the case in the business world, some stages can be skipped here, e.g. when a pressure group informs the bureaucrats directly about the outcome of their negotiations, thus by-passing the politicians. It is also possible that some stages are integrated, e.g. that the referendum democracy disappears as an independent stage. Yet again, a new and independent stage can split off (differentiation), e.g. if the executives of the political parties decide independently of their members in parliament.

The comparison of a political process with production stages makes clear that an evaluation of the separate stages is worth while only if it then becomes possible to judge how the production process functions as a whole. This is why the elements of the conversion process discussed in this book are reassembled in Chapter 7 and are then evaluated in their mutual relationship.

2

The welfare optimum

2.1 Rationality

Aim

I shall evaluate the political process from the viewpoint of the individual citizen. This I can do only if I assume that individual citizens really do have a point of view, i.e. strive to achieve a clearly defined aim. If the individuals did not strive after an aim it would be impossible to judge any organisational form against the aims of the individuals.

Weber (Rheinstein, 1954, pp. 1–2) classified human conduct as traditional, affective, value-rational and purpose-rational. Traditional social conduct is determined by custom; social conduct is determined affectively, especially emotionally, when it is guided by feelings and emotions which react to external stimuli; value-rational conduct is determined by the conscious faith in the absolute worth of the conduct as such, independent of any aim, whereas purpose-rational conduct is directed at the achievement of an aim. What is true for conduct as a whole is true for decisions in particular. According to Weber a person decides purpose-rationally if he aims to achieve certain results by his conduct. These results are the purpose of the decision.

I have already noted that it is essential to assume that individual social conduct is purpose-rational because it would otherwise be impossible to evaluate a political process from the point of view of individuals. This assumption is part of an honourable tradition in economics, and it is also used by other social sciences. For example, the social psychologists Krech, Crutchfield and Ballachey begin their book *Individual in Society* (1962) with the dictum: *human action is motivated, or goal-directed*.

The goals an individual strives after can be economic or non-economic. According to Robbins, economic goals are those of which the realisation involves the use of scarce goods which have alternative uses. All other goals are non-economic. It is possible to imagine cases in which economic and non-economic goals will conflict, e.g. a consumer's attempt to satisfy his economic needs might have a negative influence on his faith, hope and charity. However, I shall ignore this problem in the rest of the book by assuming that the attainment of economic goals will not influence the achievement of non-economic goals.

There is considerable confusion about the concept of economic goals: in many cases these goals are simply equated with the desire for a high income or for many goods and services. This confusion can be ended by distinguishing between income, wealth, utility, and economic welfare, thus largely following Hennipman (1945, pp. 78–9).

Income refers solely to the amount of money a person earns in a specific period. *Wealth*, a wider concept, refers to all the goods and services a person has obtained in this period. Wealth includes not only material goods but also the non-material services, and not only private goods but also social goods. Income and wealth are objective terms, in contrast to the next two terms which are purely subjective. *Utility* refers to the state of mind brought about by income, wealth or other economic factors. Utility is synonymous with the degree to which the needs of the individual are satisfied, insofar as this satisfaction depends on economic factors. Individual utility is thus the total of positive and negative utilities. The positive utilities include the pleasure an individual derives from all those goods which are in principle capable of satisfying human needs. The negative utilities include the costs of acquiring those goods (e.g. the loss of leisure) and the negative external effects which proceed from the actions of others (e.g. the negative effects on the environment). Whereas *utility* is limited to the welfare of one individual, *economic welfare* refers to the welfare of all individuals together. I shall return to this in the third part of this chapter.

Variables, an objective function, and a decision rule can be used to represent the way in which an individual views his utility and acts according to these views. *Variables* are changeable quantities, which the individual i regards as capable of influencing his subjective utility (U^i); for example, his consumption of m goods ($q_1^i, q_2^i, \ldots, q_m^i$) and his effort ($a^i$). An *objective function* represents the way in which variables influence utility as seen by the individual i:

$$U^i = U^i (q_1^i, q_2^i, \ldots, q_m^i; a^i)$$

If the coefficients are known, such a function provides an insight into the relative weights given by the individual to each variable. A *decision rule* is the extent to which an individual strives to realise his targets. I assume that each individual will attempt to maximise the level of his objective function: $U^i = U^i_{max}$.

Consistency

Lindblom (1968, pp. 12–28) has objected strongly to the above assumption that individuals act on the basis of an objective function. He argues that targets are never given but are continuously changing. Consequently for him, utility is a non-operational concept, the exact nature of the objective function only becomes clear when a choice is made between alternative, mutually exclusive policy programmes. Thus, targets and means are related throughout the entire process of choosing and cannot be separated.

Even when targets and means cannot be distinguished, it is possible to differentiate them for analytical purposes. The fact that a person does not know that he has an objective function does not mean that this function is non-existent. The implicit or explicit existence of an objective function is determined not only by the fact that a person aims to achieve certain goals but also that he does so consistently (Klant, 1972, pp. 95–101). First, this means that the variables are *connected*. A person must compare these variables with each other. Suppose that in a referendum a citizen first votes for stronger defence, and then for lower taxation; this may result from the fact that he has not been able to connect the levels of expenditure on defence and of taxation. In this case the goals of this citizen are inconsistent.

Consistency, however, means not only that the variables are connected, it also means *transitivity*. A person must be able to arrange the alternatives transitively, i.e. arrange them in an ordinal sequence. A citizen must be aware of the relative weight an alternative has for him so that he knows whether his utility will be increased or decreased by a change in the basket of goods. Consistency, then, requires that a person orders the alternative baskets *a* and *b* as follows:
(1) he prefers *a* to *b*, *b* to *a*, or is indifferent to *a* and *b* (requirement of connectedness), and
(2) if he prefers *a* to *b* and *b* to *c*, then he will prefer *a* to *c* (requirement of transitivity).
May (Riker and Ordeshook, 1973, pp. 16–19) gives an example of intransitive preferences among male mathematics students who were asked about their preferences among brides. The brides were

classified as to beauty, intelligence, and income. The preferences were in general as follows: 1. first, they preferred beautiful, clever but poor brides to beautiful, dumb but rich ones; 2. then, the beautiful, dumb but rich ones to ugly, clever and also rich ones; 3. finally, they preferred the ugly, clever and rich ones in their turn to the beautiful, clever but poor ones. During a lecture on these results one of my students remarked: 'True, my preference for women changes according to where I am and when', but the intransitivity in this example resulted from the fact that the students tested were unable to decide on the weight they wanted to give to each characteristic at a *single* place and at *one* point of time.

Koo (Kornai, 1971, p. 136) studied to what extent American housewives were consistent when shopping. On the basis of this study, Koo constructed a consistency-index γ, which can have a value between 0 and 1 ($0 \leqslant \gamma \leqslant 1$). If a housewife is 'steadily consistent' in her orderings $\gamma = 1$; if she is 'steadily inconsistent' $\gamma < 0.5$; if she is 'restrictedly inconsistent' $0.5 < \gamma < 1$. The numerical results of Koo's study can be summarised as follows: 1 per cent of the housewives were 'steadily consistent' in their orderings ($\gamma = 1$); 2 per cent of the housewives were 'steadily inconsistent ($\gamma < 0.5$); 86 per cent of the housewives were 'restrictedly consistent' ($0.6 < \gamma < 0.8$).

This conclusion confirms our everyday experience that most people are neither totally consistent nor totally inconsistent but that they are reasonably consistent in their orderings. The hypothesis of rationality is a hypothesis which does not apply at all times. It cannot be used to describe all orderings, but the available empirical evidence suggests that *it does apply to most orderings*.

Maximisation

An important part of the framework is the decision-rule. It is assumed that the decision-maker decides according to his preference ordering. This means that the decision-maker aims at achieving the *highest possible* utility i.e. that he tries to maximise his utility (U^i_{max}). Thus, I regard the individual citizen as a *homo economicus* who, *as soon as he knows of possibilities to improve his situation*, will no longer be content with the existing situation.

Against the assumption that people will try to maximise the level of one or more variables, Simon (1957, pp. 196–206) and his followers (Lindblom, 1968, p. 13; Kornai, 1971, p. 107) placed another assumption, that people strive only to reach a limited level of aspirations. Such a level can be, for example, an annual salary of £5,000 in combination with a 40-hour working week. A person who has reached his level of aspirations will not try to reach a higher level because all combinations of more than £5,000 and less than 40 hours are equally satisfactory.

The description of decision-rules in the form of levels of aspirations has been very popular in the social sciences and was introduced into economics by Cyert and March (1963, pp. 114–27). It provides important practical and theoretical advantages. When the rule is not formulated as 'the level of my income must rise as much as is possible' but as 'my income must amount to £5,000 per year', it becomes possible to determine unambiguously whether the goal has been achieved. Furthermore, the concept of the *level of aspirations* can also make allowance for ignorance and the complexities of the situation. This will become clear in the rest of my argument.

It must *not* be concluded from the fact that the formulation of decision-rules in the form of levels of aspiration has some advantages, that individuals *do not strive for a maximum utility*. The fallacy of such a conclusion can be shown by making a distinction between subjective and objective rationality, following Hennipman (1945, pp. 331–5; later also Simon, 1957). A decision is subjectively rational if a decision-maker attempts to bring his objective function to the highest possible level. A decision is objectively rational if the maximum that could be achieved is actually achieved. The difference between objective and subjective rationality is due, on the one hand, to incomplete information about possible behavioural alternatives and their implications, and, on the other hand, to the impossibility of digesting all information. For example, a chess player acts subjectively, not objectively, rationally: he makes his moves without considering all possible strategies, is uncertain about the consequences of each of the alternatives, and is unable to take the effects of each possible move into consideration rapidly (Simon, 1972).

Because of lack of information and the complexity of the situation, it is often impossible to achieve an objective maximum; and the achievement of an aspiration level of the desired goals will have to be sufficient. Yet, the achievement of this aspiration level does not mean that the decision-maker is really satisfied. As soon as he has more information, his aspiration level will be raised, and he will attempt to increase his utility level. The assumption that a decision-maker will maximise his utility thus means that he will, *given the information*, prefer the better to the less (assuming he is able to compare his rival preferences and to arrange them in an ordinal sequence). Riker and Ordeshook (1973, p. 23) conclude: 'Unless we ask decision makers to play God, maximizing and satisficing are the same thing.

Measuring utility

In principle there are two methods of measuring objective functions, by asking people about their goals (interview method) or by studying their actual choices (revealed preference method). These methods do not have the same value. In this book I analyse the influence exerted by the organisation of the political process on an individual's actual choice. One of my conclusions will be that some existing organisations stimulate individuals to make the 'wrong' choices, i.e. to make decisions which do not lead to the goal the individual himself wants to achieve. An attempt to draw conclusions from the preferences revealed by this 'distorted' behaviour would lead to a tautology: it is proved that existing institutions lead to 'optimum' decisions on the basis of goals defined not only by individuals but also by the institutions. The revealed preference method makes it impossible *a priori* to evaluate the existing political and economic process on the basis of the goals of individuals, so that *my problem* is best served by the interview method.

Both the interview and the revealed preference method use a number of measuring scales, of which the best known are the ordinal scale, the interval scale and the ratio scale.

A measuring scale is *ordinal* if meaning can only be given to the fact that numbers are larger or smaller. An ordinal scale is a means of indicating an order. For example, in an interview three baskets of private and collective goods are put before the respondent who is asked to value the three alternatives by means of a mark between 0 and 10. In the example, the respondent values the three alternatives with 8, 6 and 2. We can speak of an ordinal scale if we can conclude that the respondent places the highest value on the alternative with an 8, that he considers the alternative with a 6 his second choice, and values least the alternative with a 2 but that no meaning may be given to the relative differences between the three measures.

On the other hand, we speak of an *interval scale* if meaning *is* given to the difference between the numbers so that it is meaningful to add and subtract them. In the above example, there would be an interval scale if, from the marks given, the conclusion could be drawn that the differences in utility between the first and second alternative (8 minus 6) is half that between the second and third alternative (6 minus 2), but that the ratios between the figures 8, 6 and 2 have no meaning.

A *ratio scale* is an interval scale in which meaning *can* be given to the ratios, so that it is meaningful to divide and multiply. A necessary condition here is that the figure 'zero' is regarded as 'nothing'. In the example there is a ratio scale if a mark of 0 means 'no utility at all' and thus that a value of 8 means four times the utility of a value of 2. Only the unit of measurement may remain arbitrary.

In economics a distinction is also made between ordinal and cardinal methods of measuring. The ordinal method uses an ordinal scale, whereas the cardinal method (in contrast to mathematical terminology) uses an interval scale or a ratio scale.

There are three schools of thought in welfare economics as regards the measurability of individual goals. The oldest is derived from the founder of welfare economics, Pigou (1920), who, following Marshall (1890), measures utility and economic welfare by means of the 'measuring-rod of money' in which a zero outcome is considered 'no utility at all'. Even though Pigou's *oeuvre* has more examples of adding and subtracting than of multiplication and division (however, see Pigou, 1947, p. 64), his basic principle implies that he, like Marshall, regards utility as a 'cardinal' quantity which can be measured on a *ratio scale*. Paretian welfare theory has criticised this idea that utility can be measured. Pareto (1906) thought that utility can be measured on an ordinal scale only; to use his own words: 'A man can know that the third glass of wine gives him less pleasure than the second; but he can in no way tell what quantity of wine he must drink after the second glass in order to get pleasure equal to that which the second glass of wine provided him' (Pareto, 1971, p. 191).

Up to the present, Pareto's view dominates. However, since Von Neumann and Morgenstern (1944) developed an ingenious method using hypothetical interviews to measure utility on an *interval scale*,*

---

* To the mathematical student their method can be explained using the following simple example. Assume that an individual prefers a glass of tea to a cup of coffee and a cup of coffee to a glass of milk. The 'cardinal' problem of ordering these preferences is in determining the difference in utility between tea and coffee and that between coffee and milk. Von Neumann and Morgenstern obtained the answer to this question by asking the individual what he preferred: a cup of coffee or a glass which has an equal chance of containing either tea or milk. If the individual is indifferent to this choice, the utility of coffee will lie exactly midway between that of tea and milk. Another possibility is that an individual will only be indifferent to this choice if the chance that

the cardinal concept of utility has regained ground. Van Praag (1968, 1971), for example, measures the goals of households by means of a *selfrating* [interval] *scale*, on which the interviewed persons can indicate their utility on a scale between 0 and 10.

I noted that Lindblom seriously doubted whether goals could be measured, partly because they would continuously be changing and would not set until the actual choice was made. Van Praag's study has thrown new light on this matter. His results show, for example, that someone with an income of £5,000 per year will predict an increase in his utility from 5 to about 6.5 if he expects his net income to rise by £1,100. If this rise does not change the objective function, he would have continued to value his utility at 6.5. It becomes apparent that Lindblom's conclusion is valid in one respect: the objective function does change. Van Praag found that a rise in income of £1,100 in actuality will lead to a utility not of 6.5 but of about 5.4. This means that part of the increase in income, £700 in this example, does not lead to a greater utility. As soon as the income has increased, the real rise in utility is disappointing, i.e. it is on average only 35 per cent of the predicted improvement. This is a consequence of the 'preference drift': the objective function shifts along with the level of utility. It is a merit of Van Praag's work, however, that he has shown that shifts in the objective function need not detract from its usefulness.

2.2 Optimum utility

Indivisibility

My aim is to illustrate the coordinating methods of democracy and bureaucracy in the public sector of an economy. In Chapter 1, I sketched the growth of the public sector. The type of activities usually performed within the public sector are generally described in the welfare economic literature as activities with decreasing costs,

---

the glass will contain tea has risen to 60 per cent (and has consequently fallen to 40 per cent in respect of milk). In this case the 'utilities' of tea, coffee and milk have become 10, 6 and 0, or, as is easy to ascertain, 6, 4 and 1. Von Neumann and Morgenstern have found an instrument with which they can order cardinally the utilities of different alternatives by using the percentage probability at which the individual is indifferent. An interval scale is used here instead of a ratio scale because the relationship 10:6:0 differs from the relationship 6:4:1 (see also Little, 1950; 1960, pp. 34–5; Rothenberg, 1961, p. 135n. 19; Bacharach, 1976, pp. 21–2).

with external effects and intended to bring about income transfers (see, for example, Tinbergen, 1959). In order to be able to view briefly all these activities from a welfare economics point of view, I shall concentrate from now on on a special category which combines the above elements: the production of *pure social* (or *pure public*) *goods*. Scitovsky (1969, pp. 242–52), Musgrave and Musgrave (1976, pp. 50–2), Head (1972) and Millward (1971, pp. 138–41) have all put forward different characteristics to define pure social goods. I would like to summarise the common element in their analyses as follows: social goods are *goods which, once they have been provided for one individual, can be provided for others without extra costs*. This special characteristic means that one person's consumption is no rival to the consumption of another person. If one individual consumes a private good, for example an apple, then that apple cannot be eaten by anyone else. Consumption by one makes consumption by another impossible. However, if one person drives across a bridge, this in no way precludes others from driving across this bridge. Marginal production costs are, of course, incurred in the growth in the number of bridges built. But, within certain limits, no marginal consumption costs are incurred by a growth in the number of people using a particular bridge. A bridge is a consumer good which is *technically indivisible*.

Exclusion by producers

Social goods, as defined above, can be classified on the basis of two criteria, which I shall discuss in this paragraph and on page 28.

The most important criterion is the answer to the question whether the producer of a social good is able to exclude individual consumers from consuming it. In the case of some social goods it is technically possible to prevent other consumers from benefiting. This can be done by denying entry to some consumers or by charging an entrance fee, for example, a toll. Examples of this type of social goods are: roads, railways, harbours, recreation areas, fire departments and civil rights.

In the case of other social goods it is technically *im*possible to prevent other consumers from benefiting. Such goods are *inevitably* at the disposal of others as well. Well-known examples of such social goods are: lighthouses, public health, national defence, sea-walls and the ironing-out of the business cycle. A controversial example is an incomes policy *which would fall into this category if no one could be exempted from its provisions*.

Even though it is technically possible to split the first category of social goods into units which can be sold in the market, the implementation of this possibility can lead to much wastage. Once a single person is provided with such a good, it can also be made available to others at no extra cost. For as long as the use of such a good is not greater than the available capacity permits, it is efficient for all consumers to buy the social good together and to apportion the costs among themselves, instead of each individual buying the good in the market. It is thus *economically undesirable* to split such a good into saleable units.

However, in the case of the second category of social goods it is *technically impossible* to split them into saleable units, even if this would be desirable from an economic point of view. In respect of goods such as national defence and sea-walls a *quid pro quo* transaction (an exchange for a sum of money *per unit*) is ruled out in that the use of these goods cannot be made dependent on the payment of an entrance fee.

External effects

The latter category of social goods in which zero opportunity cost is combined with the impossibility of exclusion is a clear example of the more general phenomenon of *external effects*. Hennipman (1977, p. 180) defines external effects as positive or negative influences which lie outside the market and which affect the conditions of production or the level of consumption in other households. Well-known examples of external effects are the way in which some industries harm others by polluting the air and water, the obstruction of the view by a building, the traffic congestion and danger on the roads resulting from motorised vehicles, and the benefits the whole community experiences from good education and proper housing.

When the conditions of *production* in other firms are affected, the term used is 'external effects in production'; when the level of *satisfaction* in other households is affected, the term used is 'external effects in consumption'.

According to an author such as Buchanan (Millward, 1971, p. 143) external effects of consumption are present if, for example:

$$U^a = U^a(q_1^a, q_2^a, \ldots, q_m^a, q^b)$$

This means that the utility of an individual a (U^a) depends not only on his own consumption ($q_1^a, q_2^a, \ldots, q_m^a$) but also on the consumption of another individual b (q^b). This cross–dependency operates outside the market* and can be both positive and negative by nature. Positive external effects occur when *a*'s utility is positively affected by *b*'s consumption; negative effects occur when *a*'s utility is negatively affected by *b*'s consumption.

If individual *b* builds a sea-wall for his own use, *a* will inevitably benefit as well. This means that *a*'s utility is then positively influenced by *b*'s consumption. If, on the other hand, *b* plays his transistor radio too loudly, *a* will experience negative external effects.

Exclusion of the consumer

Social goods can thus be classified according to whether or not producers are able to exclude certain consumers from consuming them. Winch (1971, pp. 119–20) has suggested another classification: whether or not a consumer can choose whether he consumes the good. A consumer can decide independently whether he will drive along a certain road, enter a certain harbour or use public health services. However, he cannot decide independently whether he will be defended by a dike, an army corps, or whether or not he wishes to profit from an incomes policy or from the ironing-out of the business cycle. Once a dike is built or a business cycle ironed out, an individual consumer can in no way decide to remain unaffected.

In Table 2.1 (derived in part from Riker and Ordeshook, 1973, p. 261) social goods have been classified according to all criteria used so far. The horizontal division shows whether some consumers can be excluded from consumption by the producer of the social good. The vertical division is on the basis of whether an individual consumer can choose to consume or not. Social goods with a positive and a negative effect on utility are shown separately. For purposes of comparison not only economic but also some non-economic social goods are shown.

Samuelson calls the goods shown in the bottom right-hand corner *pure* social goods. These goods satisfy two conditions simultaneously: consumers cannot be excluded nor can they exclude themselves. All other social goods are impure, as in one form or another they all have private as well as social elements. Either the producer can limit the provision to certain individuals, or the individuals can limit their own consumption, or both.

* If external effects operate via the market mechanism, Scitovsky (Arrow and Scitovsky, 1969, pp. 242–52) and Head (1972) speak of 'pecuniary external economies'.

TABLE 2.1 *A typology of pure and impure social goods* (economic and non-economic goods)

	individuals able to choose whether or not to consume		individuals unable to choose whether or not to consume	
	utility increases by consumption	utility decreases by consumption	utility increases by consumption	utility decreases by consumption
individuals can be excluded from consumption	recreation areas harbours roads railways bridges	syphilis	fire department civil rights nationalisation	military draft nationalisation
individuals cannot be excluded from consumption	lighthouses knowledge public health	airport noise traffic congestion	incomes policy national defence sea walls counter-cyclical policy excess sunshine	incomes policy influenza environmental pollution

Samuelson has elegantly expressed the distinction between pure private goods and pure social goods in mathematical symbols:

(1) The total consumption of a pure private good, for example butter, can be divided between two persons so that one consumes less butter as the other consumes more. If Q_i is the total consumption of butter and q_i^a and q_i^b the quantities consumed by a and b respectively, total consumption equals the sum of the separate amounts consumed, i.e. $Q_i = q_i^a + q_i^b$.

(2) The total consumption of a pure social good, for example tanks, cannot be divided between two persons. Tanks are provided equally for everyone; they are consumed in their totality by everyone. If Q_k is the total consumption of cannons, and q_k^a and q_k^b are the tanks consumed by a and b, then, by definition, $Q_k = q_k^a = q_k^b$.

Optimum utility

On p. 27 I concluded on *a priori* grounds that it would be economically undesirable to split a social good into saleable units even if this were technically possible. However, this conclusion was premature because whether something is economically desirable can only be judged on the basis of an explicit criterion for optimum economic welfare. In the third part of Chapter 2, I shall attempt to formulate this criterion.

Seen from the viewpoint of a single individual it is relatively easy to define his optimum utility. The founders of public finance such as Sax and Wicksell chose as their starting point the fact that for the single individual *the positive difference between the total benefits and the total costs of social goods should be as large as possible*. On the basis of Gossen's well-known first law they assume that after the first unit of a specific social good has been consumed, each successive unit will give less satisfaction, i.e. will provide fewer benefits than the previous one. On the other hand the costs to an individual of forgoing private expenditure of his income do not weigh less heavily for each successive unit. However, as long as the benefits of the marginal unit – i.e. the least useful unit – exceed its costs, the individual's total positive balance will increase. It is only when the costs of the marginal unit exceed its benefits that the total positive balance will decrease.

According to Sax and Wicksell (Musgrave and Peacock, 1967, pp. 177–89 and 72–118) a necessary condition for achieving optimum utility is, therefore, that for the individual marginal benefits equal marginal costs. The cost of the last pound spent by the individual on contributions or taxes then just equals the benefit he receives from the last unit of the social good he consumes which was financed by this pound.

When an individual does not limit himself to one type of social good but wishes to obtain various types, the argument does not change. According to Gossen's second law, his utility will only be maximised when the costs of his marginal pound in contributions or taxes is equal in all its applications. As soon as the marginal benefits of one of the various types of social goods are no longer commensurate with the marginal pound spent on contributions or taxes, the individual would prefer to spend his marginal pound on private goods. Only when the marginal benefit and the marginal cost equal each other for each social good will an individual have reached his optimum utility, i.e. the largest possible difference between total benefits and total costs. Only then does he regard the basket of social goods provided as at an optimum.

Marshall (1890; 1961, pp. 103–7) analysed the total benefits, less total costs, for an individual, using the concept of 'consumer surplus'. When the variations in income are ignored, the benefit is expressed by the highest price an individual would, if necessary, be prepared to pay for a specific quantity of a certain good. The costs consist of the price the individual actually pays. *Thus an individual's consumer surplus is the maximum amount of money he would, if necessary, be prepared to pay for a specific quantity of a social good, less the amount of money he actually pays.*

The consumer surplus is illustrated by means of a graph in Figure 2.1 (derived in a modified form from Mishan, 1975, p. 26). This figure is based on the continually repeated question: what is the maximum amount per month an individual will, if necessary, be prepared to pay, for example, for a tank, a second tank, a third tank, etc. These amounts, which represent the marginal benefits, are shown in Figure 2.1 by the height of the successive columns. For the sake of simplicity I assume that the marginal costs of tanks remain unchanged for the individual concerned. For every extra tank the tax to be paid by him will be increased by an equal amount (P).

If an individual wishes to achieve his optimum utility then, among other things, it is essential that his marginal benefits equal his marginal costs: in this case when he has acquired 8 tanks. The maximum amount that an individual would be prepared to pay for 8 tanks is the sum of columns 1 to 8, approximately the area covered by the

Figure 2.1 *The consumer surplus of a social good for a single individual*

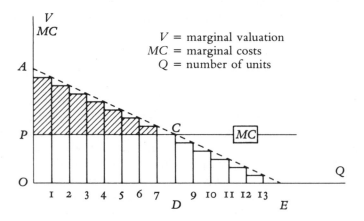

quadrilateral *ACDO*. The total amount he actually pays is shown by the oblong *PCDO*. His consumer surplus, which is at a maximum when he buys 8 tanks, is therefore the shaded part of the triangle *ACP*.

It is known that the demand for a good is determined by the quantities individuals are prepared to pay at any time at a given price. When variations in income are ignored the line *ACE* in Figure 2.1 represents the demand for a social good, in this case tanks, of the individual concerned.

2.3 Optimum economic welfare

The demand for a social good

In Figure 2.1 the line *ACE* shows the demand for a social good by *one* individual. I must now turn to the demand for a social good by *many* individuals. It is known that the total demand for a private consumer good, expressed as a quantity, equals the total of the amounts demanded by separate individuals. This is shown on the left-hand side of Figure 2.2. In this figure the curves D^a and D^b represent the demand for butter by persons a and b. The total demand for butter in this figure is the result of adding horizontally the separate demand curves ($Q^{a+b} = q^a + q^b$). Two packets of butter for 50p plus three packets for 50p after all equals five packets at 50p ($P = p^a = p^b$). On p. 30 I explained why Samuelson held that the total demand for a pure social good differs from the total demand for a pure private good. A pure social good is consumed in its totality by a as well as by b. In the example, a and b do not need to own their own tank but they can both use the same tank ($Q^{a+b} = q^a = q^b$). Adding the number of tanks demanded by a and b would therefore be misleading. *It is significant only to add the preparedness of a and of b respectively to pay a certain price for the same tank.* For example, if a is prepared to contribute £1 per week for ten tanks and b is prepared to contribute £2, then the total preparedness for ten tanks is £3 per week ($P = p^a + p^b$). This conclusion can be seen in the graph on the right-hand side of Figure 2.2. In this figure the total demand for tanks is made up of the contributions which a and b together are prepared to make for $1, 2, 3, \ldots, n$ tanks. *Thus this series is not the result of a horizontal but of a vertical addition of the separate demand curves.*

Figure 2.2 *The optimum for a private and a social good*

V = marginal benefits
MC = marginal costs
P = price
Q = quantity
q^a, q^b = quantity, individuals a, b
p^a, p^b = price, individuals a, b

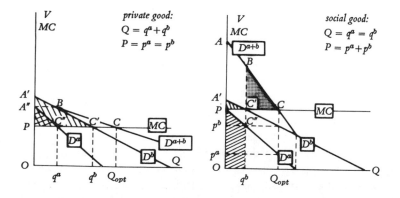

The interpersonal comparison of utility

When more than one individual is considered, it becomes difficult to define optimum welfare. After all, individuals have an endless variety of conflicting interests so that it does not necessarily follow that the goals of all individuals will be realised simultaneously. Particularly for problems of distribution, one individual's preferences may conflict with those of another individual. Welfare economics is thus concerned with how one individual's utility can be compared with that of another individual. The nature of this problem can be illustrated by an example of a canteen used by only two persons which can provide only one sort of roll. Suppose the preferences of both canteen users are arranged as in Table 2.2. These canteen users thus have conflicting preferences. Which sort of roll should be served? According to Rothenberg (1961, p. 192) and Hennipman (1977, pp. 152–72) there are, in principle, two methods of solving this problem. The first method is that of the *interpersonal evaluation of utility*. The canteen owner or the dietician can consider that ham is of greater value (e.g. healthier) than cheese, or they can be more concerned with *A*'s utility than with *B*'s. The second method is that of the *interpersonal comparison of utility*. Economists can try to provide an objective answer to the question what type of roll will ensure the greatest pleasure to the two users of the canteen, taken together, by scientifically weighing the pleasure received by *A* from a ham roll and by *B* from a cheese roll.

TABLE 2.2 *Pattern of preferences of the canteen users*

	order of preference	
Person	1	2
A	ham roll	cheese roll
B	cheese roll	ham roll

Welfare economists disagree as to whether it is possible to make interpersonal comparisons of utility. This disagreement is understandable because, as is clear in the example, the question of *comparing* utility is closely related to the question of *measuring* utility (Hennipman, 1977, pp. 157–8). An interpersonal comparison of utility is possible in the example only if the following can be determined:
(1) How many ham rolls are needed by *A* and *B* respectively to produce the same utility as one cheese roll, i.e. what is the ratio of the utility derived from ham rolls to that derived from cheese rolls (measured in defined units of utility)?
(2) What is the ratio of *A*'s unit of utility to that of *B*?
To determine (1) a *ratio scale* is essential (Riker and Ordeshook, 1973, p. 111). To determine (2) it is necessary to know the 'terms of trade' between both units of utility. *The use of a ratio scale is thus a*

necessary, but not a sufficient, condition for applying interpersonal comparisons of utility. Pareto, who considered that utility can be shown only on an ordinal scale, thus eliminated the possibility of interpersonal comparisons of utility. Pigou, on the other hand, even though he held that utility can be shown as a measurable quantity on a ratio scale, could only apply interpersonal comparisons of utility by also assuming that equal incomes provide equal utility to individuals, irrespective of their circumstances.

Economic welfare function

As already stated in Chapter 1, welfare economics is concerned not with an individual's utility but with the welfare of all individuals combined. In the first section of Chapter 2, I argued that utility can be expressed in terms of variables, an objective function and a decision rule. This also applies to the collective welfare. The collective objective function, which is also known as the *economic welfare function*, expresses the relationship between economic welfare and a number of variables which influence this economic welfare. On the basis of a decision rule it is possible to determine whether the group target has been reached.

There are three schools of thought in welfare economics and each has its own interpretation of the economic welfare function.

Pigovian welfare economics (Pigou, 1920) is based on two factors, the measurability of utility on a ratio scale and interpersonal comparisons of utility on the basis of the assumption that an equal income gives each individual the same utility. A combination of these two basic factors means that economic welfare (W) can be taken to be the sum of the separate utility of each of the n individuals:
$$W = U^1 + U^2 + U^3 + \ldots + U^n.$$
Bergsonian welfare economics (Bergson, 1966) does not give an opinion about the question of measuring utility, but rejects the possibility of making interpersonal comparisons of utility; this is replaced by an interpersonal valuation of utility on the basis of explicitly chosen ethical criteria. Thus the Bergsonian welfare function introduces the possibility of seeing economic welfare as partly dependent on the degree to which the economic targets set by political leaders have been met, irrespective of whether these targets are shared by each citizen. For example, the view on economic welfare in 1972 of the Dutch socialist leader Den Uyl has been formulated by Merkies (1973, pp. 11–27) as a welfare function of the Bergsonian type:

$$W = 0.18b + 0.34g + 0.18y + 0.12(-p) + 0.18e;$$

where

  b = increase (in billions of guilders) in the surplus on the current
      account of the *balance of payments* over the previous year;

  g = increase (in billions of guilders) in *public sector expenditure*
      over the previous year;

  y = rise (in per cent) in real disposable *income* over the previous
      year;

  $-p$ = fall (in per cent) in the *cost of living* of worker's families over
      the previous year;

  e = increase (in 10,000 man years) in the average number *em-
      ployed* over the previous year.

Paretian welfare economics rejects both the Pigovian and the Bergsonian starting points. Utility can be measured only on an ordinal
scale, comparisons of utility are economically impossible and valua-
tions of utility are without significance from an economic viewpoint. If a group strives for economic welfare this striving is expressed by a non-specified economic welfare function in which
economic welfare is seen as being exclusively dependent on the
utility of the individuals:

$$W = W(U^1, U^2, U^3, \ldots, U^n)$$

Paretian welfare economics gained greatly in importance after the
1930s. This growth was based not so much on the Paretian welfare
function as on the Paretian decision rule, which makes it possible to
avoid judging the distribution of utility and to draw conclusions
which are valid for all distributions of utility.

The Pareto criterion

Pareto (1971, p. 261), to avoid conclusions about the desired distribution of utility, formulated a criterion for economic welfare
about which a consensus among the members of a group is not *a
priori* excluded. *The Pareto criterion states that economic welfare can be
said to have increased when one or more members of the group concerned are
better off and no one is worse off*. The criterion is not only a standard for
detecting an increase in economic welfare but also for determining
how long such an increase can go on for. According to the criterion,
economic welfare is at an optimum as soon as it is no longer possible
to increase the level of utility of one or more individuals without
reducing the utility of one or more other individuals.

  A number of objections, both theoretical and practical, have been
raised against this criterion (e.g. Nath, 1969; Rowley and Peacock,

1975). Hennipman (1976, pp. 39–69) has refuted the most important theoretical objections and has shown that they are often based on the misunderstanding that the criterion of Pareto contains a *value judgment*. Many critics wrongly interpret the Pareto criterion as a norm ('it is a good thing to make one man better off if nobody else is made worse off') or more strongly, as a commandment ('no one should be made worse off'). Pareto himself (e.g. 1971, p. 2) never tired of denying that he wanted to give recipes for achieving the highest possible degree of happiness, benefit or well-being instead of an ethically neutral criterion for judging economic efficiency.

Value judgments about increases in economic welfare cannot be made without knowing which social groups benefit from the increase. If, for example, only those individuals with relatively high incomes were to profit from an increase in economic welfare, the effect would be to widen income differences and this might result in the increase being rejected even though perhaps the Pareto criterion had been fulfilled. The application of the conclusion based on the Pareto criterion must therefore always be weighed against the value judgment underlying a certain *distribution criterion*.

Hennipman (1976, p. 49) holds that a Paretian optimum cannot be regarded even from the economic point of view as the proper target. This argument can easily lead to the misunderstanding that the Pareto criterion determines which events are 'economically' desirable, even though they may be 'politically' undesirable. The critics who reject the conclusion drawn from the Pareto criterion after weighing the rival goals, act equally soundly from an economic point of view as do those who accept the outcome of the criterion.

The practical objections to the Pareto criterion concern the problem that changes in economic welfare which comply with the criterion do not often occur. Nearly every improvement in utility for some individuals is associated with a fall in utility for other individuals. In order to meet this objection, the later literature, building on the pioneering work of Kaldor and Hicks, has formulated the neo-Paretian criterion which is also known as the *compensation principle*. The neo-Paretians argue that the gainers from economic change *can* compensate the losers. They do not argue that the losers *must* be compensated because such a requirement would imply an interpersonal evaluation or comparison of utility whereas the Pareto criterion was formulated to avoid doing this (Hennipman, 1977, p. 141). The neo-Paretians merely establish that if the gain from a certain change in economic welfare is so big for the gainers that they will not only be able to compensate the losers for their loss, but still be better off, then there will be a *potential* increase in economic welfare on the basis of the Pareto criterion.

In order to determine unambiguously whether there is such a potential increase in economic welfare Scitovsky (1969, pp. 390–401) suggests that two 'compensation tests' be performed. In the first test gainers are asked whether they will be prepared to compensate the losers for the loss they will incur as a result of the change. In the second test the losers are asked whether they are prepared to compensate the gainers if the change does not take place. Should the first test have a positive result and the second test a negative result, then it cannot be said that economic welfare *will be* increased by the change, but that it is *possible*, on the basis of the Pareto criterion, that the change would increase economic welfare.

The economic welfare optimum

The Pareto criterion helped Samuelson (1954) to make general statements on the optimum economic welfare of a large number of individuals insofar as this economic welfare depends on a large number of dissimilar social goods. As Samuelson's model, in both its algebraic and its graphical form, is needlessly complicated *for my purposes*, I shall base my argument on the simpler model presented by Richard and Peggy Musgrave (1976, pp. 53–5 and 74–7). I shall limit myself to the case of two individuals and a single homogeneous private good and a single homogeneous social good.

Let us first consider the (economic welfare) optimum for two individuals and one *private good* – butter. As the marginal cost of butter equals P, it becomes possible to see from the left-hand side of Figure 2.2 that the individuals a and b reach their optimum utility when they consume q^a and q^b packets of butter, in both cases at price P per packet. At these points the marginal benefits for both a and b are equal to the marginal costs, so that for each individual the consumer surplus is at a maximum, that is, equal to the shaded areas of the triangle $A''C''P$ (for a) and of the triangle $A'C'P$ (for b).

Assume that there is an omniscient and benevolent dictator (e.g. the philosopher–king in Plato's *Republic*) who decides on the level of output of the good and its distribution between a and b. Assume also that the philosopher–king decides that the total quantity of butter produced will amount to Q_{opt} at a price P per packet. Thus this point represents a potential optimum (in neo-Paretian terminology), because the total consumer surplus is at a maximum, viz. equal to the area covered by the square $A'BCP$. This point also represents a real optimum in Paretian terms provided total consumption is divided among a and b so that a consumes q^a and b consumes q^b. After all, such a division means that everyone's individual position is at an optimum and the king cannot improve the position of either individual without worsening the position of the other.

This argument applies, by analogy, to the (economic welfare) optimum of two individuals and a *social good* – a tank. Assume that the marginal costs of tanks equal OP, then it is possible to read from the right-hand side of Figure 2.2 that when there is no group action, individual a will be at an optimum when he does not buy a single tank and b's optimum will be reached at q^b tanks. The marginal benefits of a and b equal their marginal costs at these points. Thus q^b tanks are bought from which both a and b will profit. The consumer surplus of a then equals the shaded quadrilateral $PC''q^bO$ (since he pays nothing for the tank) and that of b will equal the shaded area of the triangle $A'C'P$. The total consumer surplus then equals the area $ABC'P$, that is, equals the total benefit (the area ABq^bO) minus total costs (the area $PC'q^bO$).

Assume once again that a philosopher–king decides on the level of output and the distribution of the social good. Assume also that the king decides that Q_{opt} tanks are produced at a price P per tank. Thus this point represents a potential optimum because the total consumer surplus is at a maximum, viz. equals the whole area of the triangle ACP. The actions of the philosopher–king have thus increased the total consumer surplus by the dotted triangle BCC'. The potential optimum can be transformed into a real optimum by dividing the total costs between a and b so that a contributes p^a, and b contributes p^b per cannon. Such a division thus provides each individual with an optimum position and the king can improve the position of the one only by worsening that of the other.

Thus, the economic welfare optimum for a social good has the following characteristics:

(1) The individuals (a and b) contribute so that for each individual the marginal benefits equal that individual's marginal costs.
(2) The total contributions of the individuals (a and b) combined equal the total costs of the social good.
(3) The sum of the marginal benefits of the individuals (a and b) equal the marginal costs of the social good.

In summary, I conclude that the (economic welfare) optimum for private goods differs in at least two respects from that for social goods. In an optimum situation, (pure) private goods are consumed in different quantities by different consumers at the same price, but (pure) social goods are consumed in the same quantity by different consumers at different prices. The optimum for private goods means that *for each* consumer separately the marginal benefits equal the marginal costs of the good. However, the optimum for social goods means that their marginal benefits, *which represent the sum of the marginal benefits of all consumers*, equal the marginal costs of the good. The market mechanism is thus, under certain circumstances, capable of producing the optimum quantity of private goods but not of public goods. Insofar as economic welfare depends on social goods the economic welfare optimum can only be obtained by an institution capable of adding the marginal benefits of individuals. In the following chapters a number of such institutions will be examined, viz. negotiations democracy, referendum democracy, representative democracy and bureaucracy. All these institutions are logical stages in the conversion of individual needs into social goods which I have termed the *political process*.

3

Negotiation

3.1 Negotiations democracy

Freedom of exit and non-commitment

In Chapter 2, I considered what conditions had to be met if economic welfare is to be at an optimum. I discussed this optimum welfare from the viewpoint of a philosopher–king who stands aside from politics. I did not discuss the question whether this optimum can be realised in practice and if so under what institutional conditions. These conditions will be examined in Chapters 3 to 6. In this chapter on *negotiations democracy* I shall consider whether groups whose members negotiate with each other with freedom of exit and without commitment are able to achieve that policy which will provide an optimum economic welfare for the members of the group. It is important to introduce the concept of a group since in an analysis all collective acts are performed by or on behalf of a group, because a system of individual transactions for buying social goods on a free market is not appropriate. *Freedom of exit* means that the members are free to leave the group. *Non-commitment* means that group decisions do not bind the individual members. Examples of such groups, based more or less on freedom of exit and non-commitment, are: action groups, trade unions, military alliances (e.g. NATO in times of peace) and international organisations (the United Nations).

The study of a negotiations democracy is important for two reasons. First, a negotiations democracy is an independent decision-making model which occurs fairly frequently. Kirschen (1968, p. 187) has even characterised our whole economic order as an *'économie concertée'*, i.e. as a negotiations democracy in which the government takes its decisions in 'concerted action' with organised pressure groups, especially employers' organisations and trade unions, which are in no way obliged to cooperate. Secondly, group negotiations are an important element in every democratic political process. An analysis of the negotiations is therefore necessary in order to understand the way in which the whole process functions.

Self-interest and 'class interest'

In this book it is assumed that the members of a group make 'subjective rational' decisions. As was explained in Section 2.1 this assumption merely means that the individual members of a group:

– strive to achieve their own goal;
– see this goal as maximising their utility which, among other things, depends on the group's decision on goods and services;
– are able to compare the various alternatives and to order them transitively;
– decide according to their preference ordering.

Mancur Olson in his book, *The logic of collective action* (1965; 1971), provided the first consistently formulated and systematic analysis of the economic theory of groups. In this book Olson defined groups as *a number of individuals with a 'common interest'* (1971, p. 8), i.e. a number of individuals who strive partly after the same *individual goal*. This concept goes back to the classical economists. Marx, too, based his definition of 'class' not on irrational social ties between the members, but on economic factors. He distinguished between a 'Klasse an sich' (a class as such) and a 'Klasse für sich' (a class for itself). The former is determined by the relations of production. Those who own factors of production are members of the 'capitalist class' while the others make up the 'proletariat'. In the Marxist view the members of a class become conscious of their class at a certain moment. The capitalists strive to expropriate the 'surplus value' formed during the process of production, and the exploited proletariat will begin to resist. The classes 'as such' then become classes 'for themselves': both classes will then be characterised by their aims in the production process.

Marx had a great contempt for those socialists who believed that human behaviour was based on an inborn altruism. Together with Engels he wrote in the *Manifesto of the Communist Party*:

The history of all hitherto existing society is the history of class struggles.
    The modern bourgeois society that has sprouted from the ruins of feudal society has not done away with class antagonisms. It has but established new classes, new conditions of oppression, new forms of struggle in place of the old ones.
    It [the bourgeoisie] has pitilessly torn asunder the motley feudal ties that bound man to his natural superiors, and has left remaining no other nexus

between man and man than naked self-interest . . . It has drowned the most heavenly ecstasies of religious fervour, of chivalrous enthusiasm, of philistine sentimentalism, in the icy water of egotistical calculation.

Marx regarded ideology as a cloak for self-interest. He ridiculed the Church of England in his remark that it would pardon an attack on 38 of its 39 Articles of Religion more readily than it would an attack on 1/39th of its income.

The stress Marx laid on rational behaviour led to much criticism. For example, the sociologist Wright Mills (1951, pp. 325–8) argued that in Marx's view class action will always come about if the members of a class are rationally aware of: (a) the interests of their own class; (b) the interests of other classes; (c) the fact that the interests of the other classes are illegitimate; (d) the possibilities of using collective political action. Repeating Veblen (1919) he concludes: 'This idea is just as rationalist as liberalism in its psychological assumptions.' This idea is indeed 'utilitarian and more closely related to Bentham than Hegel' for it is based on 'a calculus of advantage'. The error of this Marxist view has long been proved, according to Wright Mills, by the widespread political apathy. He concludes: 'Indifference . . . is the major sign of the . . . collapse of socialist hopes.'

However, Olson (1971, pp. 105–10) defends Marx against Veblen and Wright Mills. He agrees with Marx's assumption that every class action is based on a cost–benefit analysis. Yet, in his opinion Marx made one fundamental error in logic. When the members of the proletariat strive to further their personal interests in a rational manner, then, in the Marxist view, this means that the proletarian *class* will also strive rationally to further its own interests. Thus, an 'invisible hand' will achieve a harmony between individual and class optima. However, Olson learned from Wicksell's theory that it was incorrect to make such an implicit assumption. When it is assumed that an individual will serve his own self-interest, it may not be assumed *a priori* that he will also serve the interests of his class. This can be seen from Marx's own example of the 'capitalist class': the entrepreneurs. These entrepreneurs strive after the same goal: maximising profits. As is known (in neo-classical theory) the realisation of this goal-directed striving by individual entrepreneurs results in the group making no profit at all. The individual's striving after profits means an accumulation of decisions to expand production so that the market price will fall to the point where profits disappear. In this case, the individual optimum conflicts with the collective optimum. What is true for the entrepreneurs might also be true for the proletariat. It would be logically inconsistent to accept the possibility of conflicts between the individual and the collective optimum in the case of entrepreneurs but to deny its likelihood, *a priori*, in the case of the proletariat.

Exchange

The residents of a district, the inhabitants of a town, the citizens of a country, or the workers in a trade union can all be seen as members of a group. As the members of such a group strive partly to achieve a number of similar goals, they can try to achieve an optimum result for the whole group by means of multilateral negotiations in which exit by the group members is free and participation does not commit them further than they wish to go. Later in this chapter it will be shown that in some cases it is not possible to achieve an optimum result for the group by this type of negotiation. But that conclusion can be understood only when it is clear why an optimum *can* be reached in other circumstances.

Lindahl (1919; 1967), Johansen (1965, pp. 123–53) and Buchanan (1968, pp. 11–48) have shown in what circumstances a collective optimum can be reached by means of negotiations and exchange in which participation allows for freedom of exit and does not require further commitment. There are five elements in the process of negotiation they describe. First, the negotiators must operate from positions of about equal power. Secondly, *simultaneous* negotiations are held by all the citizens with each other on the nature of the social goods and on each citizen's share in the costs. Thirdly, the costs are shared in such a way that a small share for one person means a large share for someone else. In the fourth place, the individual's demand curve falls (see Figure 2.1 on page 32) which means that an individual's demand for social goods increases as his price, i.e. his share in the costs per unit, decreases. In the fifth place, the behaviour of every negotiator during the negotiations is 'Pareto efficient', i.e. he is prepared to allow an improvement in the position of the other party on condition that his own position does not deteriorate.

Of course, such a process of negotiations will occur only occasionally in real life. Yet it is necessary to discuss this abstraction because it will enable us, by gradually reducing the degree of abstraction, to gain an insight into decision-making by groups in real life.

In the model used by Lindahl and others the process of negotiation between each pair of individuals *a* and *b* has the following pattern. If

a's share in costs per unit is, at first, low, then he will desire many units, i.e. a high level of social goods. Then b's share in the costs per unit is high so that he will want few units, i.e. a low level of social goods. Person a will then offer to reduce b's share in the costs per unit in order to persuade b to accept more social goods. On the other hand, if b initially has a relatively small share in the costs per unit, the roles will be reversed. However disparate the original positions chosen for a and b, somewhere 'in the middle' there will be a point (the share in the costs per unit and the subsequent level of social goods) at which a and b will meet and which will satisfy two conditions, viz. the costs and benefits of each individual will be in equilibrium, and the position of at least one of the two will have improved without any deterioration in the position of the other. When a and b have arrived at a consensus, they will together negotiate with c until agreement has been reached. The process will be repeated until a point has been reached where individuals arc in equilibrium.

The negotiations between a and b thus lead to an exchange between them. Buchanan has succeeded in giving an acceptable graphic representation of how such an exchange takes place using traditional supply and demand curves, excluding variations in income. In Figure 3.1, D^a and D^b are the same demand curves as were shown on the right-hand side of Figure 2.2. (page 33) representing the demand of a and b, for example for tanks. If a and b were to act completely independently, a would abstain from buying and b would buy q^b tanks from which a, too, would benefit. Thus both consume q^b but a consumes this quantity without having to pay anything at all. The opportunity for an exchange now exists which will be advantageous to both. Buchanan demonstrates this possibility by asking the question: What price must b receive from a before he is prepared to buy yet more tanks? And, alternatively: What price is a prepared to pay b to induce b really to buy these tanks? When both questions yield the same answer, then it is advantageous to both to buy more tanks in exchange for a higher share in the costs made by a.

Buchanan bases the answer to the first question, viz. what b wants to receive, on the fact that b, too, wants more tanks than q^b as can be seen from his demand curve D^b. To buy yet more tanks b must receive at least the negative *difference* between his marginal benefits of these tanks and his marginal costs. It is therefore possible to draw a supply curve S^b, which will show the extra tanks that b will buy in addition to his initial quantity q^b.

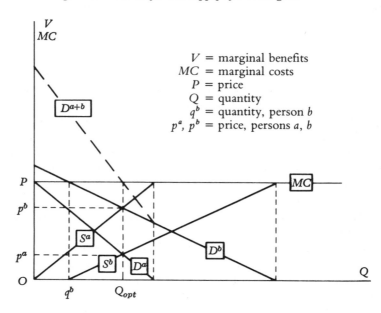

Figure 3.1 *Demand for and supply of a social good*

Buchanan has based the answer to the second question, viz. what a is prepared to pay for more tanks on the marginal benefits which a will get from the extra tanks. The marginal benefits of each arbitrary number of tanks is shown graphically by a's demand curve. The costs per tank which a is prepared to pay for the purchase of more than q^b tanks is shown in that part of the demand curve D^a to the right of point q^b.

The number of extra tanks b offers equals the number requested by a at the point where S^b cuts D^a. At this point b exchanges his willingness to buy Q_{opt} tanks instead of q^b tanks for a's preparedness to pay p^a for each extra tank instead of paying nothing.

I assumed that b buys the extra tanks and that a contributes to their cost. Of course, the roles of a and b can be reversed in which case curve S^a represents the willingness of a to buy tanks and D^b the price b is prepared to pay per tank. The point where S^a and D^b cut is where Q_{opt} tanks are bought whereas b pays p^b for each tank.

The Dutch saying 'waar er twee ruilen, moet er één huilen' (in any swop there is a gainer and a loser) does not often apply to voluntary exchanges, viz. exchanges made without coercion, error or fraud. On the assumption that the parties in an exchange negotiate from positions of more or less equal power, Lindahl, Johansen and Buchanan have shown that by exchanges the results for both *a* and *b* can improve. Political phenomena such as 'horse trading', compromising, and forming coalitions are not *a priori* inconsistent with the ambition to achieve a higher economic welfare. On the contrary, exchanges often make it possible to achieve a higher level of economic welfare than would otherwise have been the case. There are cases in which a greater level of satisfaction for one party by no means makes satisfaction for the other party impossible.

The Prisoners' Dilemma

The model discussed in the previous paragraph is based on a large number of assumptions, the first two of which are the most important. The assumption that *a* and *b* negotiate from positions of equal power means that a *democratic* process of negotiations is being discussed. However, many processes are autocratic by nature. The assumption that simultaneous negotiations are held between all members of the group on the nature of the social goods and each member's share in the costs, is even more unrealistic. At most, this assumption applies to small groups, i.e. groups consisting of only a few persons. In large groups most members will make their decisions more or less in isolation. A well-known example of this can be found in the price theory. In an oligopoly (few suppliers) each firm, when fixing its prices, will (have to) take the reactions of its competitors into account. In a situation of perfect competition (many suppliers) an individual will regard the price of his competitors as given and will adapt accordingly. In the first case the firm will regard its own price as having an influence on the prevailing market prices. In the second case, however, a firm will assume that its own price has no influence on the market price whatsoever.

The representatives of the pressure groups who negotiate in a negotiations democracy with each other and with the government áre, in themselves, a small group. Yet these pressure groups are not monoliths, but are composed of many members who all strive after their own goals. Precisely because of the nature of the process of negotiations (freedom of exit and non-commitment), the members do not regard themselves as bound by the outcome. The fringe members, especially, will determine independently whether or not they will accept the policy of the group representatives and the latter are, in turn, compelled to take this fact into proper account. Thus, in practice, a large number of people are involved, both directly and indirectly, in the process of decision-making. This makes Lindahl's assumption that all persons negotiate simultaneously with each other unrealistic. In the large groups of a negotiations democracy, each person will assume that his own contribution to the decision-making process will have no influence on the outcome.

The consequences of this assumption will be considered in the remainder of this chapter, using *Game Theory*. A *game* is a (mathematical) simulation of human behaviour, in which a logical relationship is made between the individuals' or groups' aims, their behaviour and the results they achieve. The individuals or groups, whose behaviour is being analysed, are called *players*. The way in which a player will act in a given situation is called a *strategy*. The results of a strategy are termed *outcome*, and this outcome is evaluated on the basis of the *utility* that the players experience.

According to the number of individuals participating in the (simulated) game a distinction is made, among other things, between two-person and *n*-person games. In addition, the games are divided into: zero-sum games and nonzero-sum games (often positive-sum games). A *zero-sum game* can be defined as a game in which the interests of the players are diametrically opposed so that the one's profit equals the other's loss. *Nonzero-sum games* are games in which the players have some common interests. The process of exchange described by Lindahl (pp. 44–45 is an example of a nonzero-sum game because more utility for one player does not prevent the other player from increasing his utility.

The consequences of the fact that individuals in a large group have no influence on the outcome of the decision-making process can best be explained using a two-person positive-sum game known as the *Prisoners' Dilemma Game* (Luce and Raiffa, 1957, pp. 94ff). The name is derived from a game, devised by the American mathematician A. W. Tucker, in which two prisoners together committed a crime which has not yet been proved. Tucker also assumes that:
– if no proof is provided, the men will be kept on remand for one year, after which they will be released;
– if one prisoner turns Queen's or State's evidence, he will be released immediately but the other, who kept silent, will be given a life (i.e. a thirty-year) sentence;
– if both prisoners confess, each will be sent to prison for fifteen years.

Table 3.1 gives an outcome matrix showing clearly the various possibilities, expressed in terms of the prison sentence. On the basis of this outcome matrix, a *pay-off matrix* has been drawn (Table 3.2). A pay-off matrix shows the effects of various alternatives on the players' utility. If the effects on utility can be measured ordinally and the players always prefer a short prison sentence to a long one, then the four alternatives under discussion can be given the utility values 4, 3, 2 and 1, in which 4 is the most preferred and 1 the least preferred. In the pay-off matrix shown here the first figure always refers to *a*'s utility, the second to *b*'s.

TABLE 3.1 *Prisoners' Dilemma: outcome matrix*

		prisoner *b*	
		silence	confession
prisoner *a*	silence	$(-1; -1)$ *a* *b*	$(-30; 0)$ *a* *b*
	confession	$(0; -30)$ *a* *b*	$(-15; -15)$ *a* *b*

TABLE 3.2 *Prisoners' Dilemma: pay-off matrix*

		prisoner *b*	
		silence	confession
prisoner *a*	silence	(3;3) →	(1;4)
	confession	(4;1) →	(2;2)

The pay-off matrix shows that both prisoners have a common interest in keeping silent so that they will only have to undergo a short period on remand. In this case they will both achieve their second priority (3;3) which is also a Paretian optimum because it is impossible to increase one prisoner's utility without reducing that of the other. Each prisoner also has an individual interest in turning Queen's evidence, so that:
– (if the other keeps silent) he will be released immediately (1;4) or (4;1);

– (if the other also confesses) he reduces his sentence to fifteen years instead of receiving a life (or thirty year) term (2;2).

When both prisoners are isolated from each other so that they cannot influence each other's decision, we can predict that both will confess and provide proof of the other's complicity. Dror (1968, p. 152) concludes wittily: 'As a result, both rational prisoners will spend fifteen years in prison thinking about the limitations of pure rationality.' The Prisoners' Dilemma, however, does not prove that 'extra-rational decision-making processes are demonstrably better than pure rationality' as Dror suggests, but merely that *individual rationality does not necessarily lead to social rationality in those cases in which individuals are unable to influence each other's decision.*

The problem illustrated by the Prisoners' Dilemma can be formulated more sharply. It is in the common interest of both prisoners to agree to a *cooperative* strategy. In Table 3.2 this is the strategy that has as its result the Paretian optimum (3;3). This cooperative strategy does not lead to an *equilibrium.* For the non-cooperative strategy is *dominant* because each player will want to choose it irrespective of his opponent's strategy. If his opponent chooses a cooperative strategy, he will choose a non-cooperative strategy so as to realise his first priority (four utility points) instead of his second priority (three utility points). Should his opponent choose a non-cooperative strategy he will do the same in order to achieve his third priority in preference to his fourth priority. As a result, both prisoners will, despite their common interest, choose a non-cooperative strategy and achieve a result (2;2) which is not a Paretian optimum. In Table 3.2 arrows are used to show how the players choose their strategies. The vertical arrows show the direction in which player *a* changes his strategic behaviour and the horizontal arrows show how player *b* will change his strategic behaviour. The outcome is self-evident.

3.2 Negotiations democracy and economic welfare

Political participation and economic welfare

In the previous section much emphasis was laid on the fact that most negotiations which take place in a negotiations democracy are within a large, not a small group. In a large group the individual has no personal relationship with the other people. Most people will assume that their individual contribution to the decision-making process will have a negligible effect on the outcome.

Olson (1965; 1971) has asked what this means for the *participation* of individuals in the decision-making process. As I have already mentioned (p. 43), he thinks that the individual's decision to participate or not depends on a subjective rational weighing of individual costs and benefits. Independent of Olson, this view is also accepted by the sociologist Lammers (1973) who concludes from a study of participation in the decision-making process at Dutch universitites, which have a democratic internal structure, that:

People . . . often assume, quite gratuitously, that
1. the same group always participates;
2. non-participation is always a sign of aversion or alienation.
As I have shown from the available data . . . neither assumption is necessarily true . . . This is a result of the fact that non-participation often occurs because a member or voter feels that things carry on well enough without him. This is a form os positive apathy. One doesn't participate – this time – because one feels one can rely on the fact that those who do participate . . . will arrive at a reasonably acceptable decision and because one is able to use the time to do something else which is more . . . enjoyable. However, as soon as members must decide on far-reaching matters, or, in general, when the organisation is in a critical situation, then a sort of mobilisation takes place and as a result those already active become more active and the lukewarm become less passive.

Even though Olson views participation much more pessimistically than Lammers, he, too, assumes that those who do not participate sponge on those who do. His argument can best be given not by quoting it, but by expressing it in terms of a Prisoners' Dilemma. An individual voter in a large group can argue in two ways:
(1) the voter assumes that, even if he himself does not participate, the policy he supports will be realised by others;
(2) the voter assumes that, even if he does participate, the others will not help to realise the policy he supports.
The first assumption leads to what Lammers calls 'positive apathy'. As soon as a voter feels that, after all, others will realise the desired policy, it is only to his advantage to keep himself aloof.
The second assumption, too, leads to apathy but in this case it is a 'negative apathy'. When others will not cooperate to achieve the desired policy, it is often not worthwhile for the individual voter to participate. Or, as Lammers might say 'When others have no sound policy, it is a waste of one's time to try to change things'.
Whatever assumption the voter may make, he will not participate in this model unless he considers the outcome of the group's decision-making to be very important or unless he regards participa-

tion as a very important *private* good, for example, because participation gives him power, prestige or social contracts.

According to Olson, Marx assumed wrongly that rational behaviour of the proletariat would lead to mass participation. Large numbers of the proletariat will sponge on the active participation of a small group because they regard the collective optimum as subservient to their individual optimum.

With Marx the wish was father to the thought: he thought that mass participation would provide an optimum for the proletariat as a whole. This was also the opinion of the 'neo-democrats' (New Left socialism, radical liberalism), who were rising in the Netherlands in the 1960s. This movement was concerned about the political apathy prevailing among the ordinary citizens: it blamed the social structure or the political system for this state of affairs. In their opinion a social optimum could be achieved only when all members of the group participated in the decision-making process, i.e. if the process described by Lindahl and his followers (*a* negotiates with *b*, *a* and *b* negotiate with *c*, etc.) were real. The pleas of the neo-democrats for a greater participation were so urgent that the Dutch political scientist Daalder (1974a, pp. 70–8) accused them of elevating the principle of participation to an absolute norm.

Seen from the point of view of welfare economics, this reproach has some justification. After all, from Olson's model it can be concluded that, if the policy is at an optimum, participation will be very small. Many voters then feel that things are well managed without them. In the case of positive apathy described above, there is no inconsistency between mass non-participation and the achievement of an economic welfare optimum.

On the basis of Olson's model it can also be predicted, however, that if the policy is far removed from the optimum, there will also be a very small participation. Many voters feel that their individual contribution to politics will not be able to turn the tide. It is clear that this case of negative apathy will by no means contribute to the achievement of a Paretian economic welfare optimum.

When applying this economic theory of participation to practical problems it is necessary to bear in mind the limits placed on economics listed in the first chapter (pp. 4 and 8). Economic theory cannot explain all social phenomena. Olson's participation theory cannot explain or even predict occurrences such as the mass mobilisations, for example, in China in 1958–59 and 1966–68, the general strike during the Second World War in February 1941 in Holland, and the violent student demonstrations in 1968–69. However, such mass participation occurs very seldom, and does not last long. Olson has, in my opinion, given an adequate description of behaviour patterns in normal times.

Collective action and economic welfare

Without saying it in so many words, Olson (1971, p. 100) pointed out a clear relationship between his own theory of participation and Wicksell's earlier theory on parasitical behaviour with respect to social goods (Musgrave and Peacock, 1967, pp. 72–118). This relationship is possible because, up to a certain point, participation is a social good: the participant is unable to exclude some citizens from the effects of his participation, nor can these citizens exclude themselves; when one citizen participates the effects of his participation are inevitably available to the other citizens (Breton, 1974, p. 98). What is true for the particular case of participation applies to social goods in general, as we shall see.

I want to illustrate the provision of social goods on the basis of freedom of exit and non-commitment, which characterises a negotiations democracy, using a simple two-person game in which negotiations are held on whether a typically Dutch social good should be provided, viz. a sea-wall (like the closing of the Oosterschelde river). I shall assume that both players will be motivated by self-interest and that this self-interest has two components: the *collective* interest in building a sea-wall and the *individual* interest in paying as little as possible. In order to make the example as realistic as possible I shall also assume that one of the players is a representative of the employees who will have to decide on whether they will forgo a part of their wages to enable the sea-wall to be built, and that the other player is a representative of the employers who must consider whether they will relinquish part of their profits to make the sea-wall possible. Finally, I shall assume that both representatives have got a free hand from their supporters.

In the example, both groups (trade unionists and employers) will benefit equally from the sea-wall so that for both groups the benefits will amount to £1.5 billion. The total costs of the sea-wall will amount to £2 billion. If the costs are divided equally between employers and trade unionists, each group will have to contribute £1 billion.

If both the trade unionists and the employers agree jointly to contribute to the sea-wall (by cutting the rate of growth of wages and profits respectively), then the total benefits will amount to £3 billion and the total costs to £2 billion, so that the net benefit will be £1 billion, or £0.5 billion per group (Table 3.3, top left). If one of the two groups were to contribute and the other to refrain from contributing, then the total costs of the sea-wall would fall on the group that contributes, which would then have a net loss of £0.5 billion while the other, non-contributing group would benefit to an amount of £1.5 billion (Table 3.3, top right and bottom left). If neither party contributes, the costs and the benefits are both zero (Table 3.3, bottom right).

TABLE 3.3 *Net benefits for trade unionists and employers* (in billions of pounds)

		trade unionists (T)			
		positive decision		negative decision	
employers (E)	positive decision	+ 0.5 E	+ 0.5 T	− 0.5 E	+ 1.5 T
	negative decision	+ 1.5 E	− 0.5 T	0 E	0 T

It is important to note that in Table 3.3. three outcomes satisfy the Paretian optimum criterion, viz. top left (0.5; 0.5), top right (−0.5; 1.5) and bottom left (1.5; −0.5). In none of these cases can the benefits of one group be increased without reducing those of another group. In all three cases the sum of the net benefit equals £1 billion; the only difference between the three possibilities lies in the way in which the net benefits are divided between the two groups. However, the net benefits in the situation shown at the bottom right (0;0) are not at an optimum. Yet this non-optimum result is the outcome of the game.

The trade unionists can base their decision on one of two assumptions:

(1) The employers decide to contribute to the project by moderating their profits (positive decision);

(2) the employers decide not to contribute (negative decision).

If the employers decide positively, then it is in the interest of trade unionists to decide negatively. After all, their net benefits will then rise from 0.5 (top left) to 1.5 (top right). If the employers decide negatively then this will mean that the trade unionists will also decide negatively. Their net benefits will then rise from −0.5 (bottom left) to 0 (bottom right). *Thus, the trade unionists will decide negatively in all cases.* In this example, the trade unions themselves are willing to sponge on the readiness of the employers to make sacrifices, but they are not prepared to accept the employers sponging on their liberality. *Mutatis mutandis*, the employers will make the same calculation: they, too, will decide negatively in all cases. The employers themselves are prepared to be 'free riders' in the trade union train, but at the same time they refuse to offer a lift to the trade unionists in their limousine.

Both trade unionists and employers will achieve a worse result than if they had cooperated. The common interest requires that one of the three Paretian optima will be reached, but in fact none of these optima is reached: trade unionists and employers each decide separately not to contribute, i.e. not to cut the rate of growth of their wages or profits. *Here there is no invisible hand which brings the self-interest of one individual into harmony with the self-interest of another individual.*

The above example is unrealistic in at least one respect. The negotiations were between only two 'individuals', viz. one representative of the employees and another of the employers, who both held *carte blanche* from their supporters. Thus both individuals are oligopolists and they will take into account the fact that their behaviour will influence the final outcome. Each negotiator will realise that a unilateral refusal to participate in the costs of the sea-wall will not mean that the other will then bear all the costs, but that the sea-wall will not be constructed at all. In such cases, it is probable that they will cooperate.

In actual fact, however, large numbers of employers and employees are engaged in the negotiations. The theory of economic behaviour in large groups can now be applied. The individual employer or employee who negotiate assumes that his individual decision whether to contribute or not will not influence the provision of the social good. However, it is now that the Prisoners' Dilemma comes into its own, provided that the game is not played between two individuals but between a single individual on the one hand and all the other individuals on the other hand. In respect of social goods an individual citizen (an employee, an employer, a shop-keeper, a housewife, a pensioner) has two possibilities in negotiations democracy:

(1) the individual assumes that the social good will be paid for by others even if he himself does not contribute to its cost;
(2) the individual assumes that the others will not contribute to the cost of the social good even if he himself does contribute.

Wicksell has already dealt with the first assumption. As soon as an individual feels that the other will pay for the social good anyhow, it is in his own interest to keep his own contribution as small as possible. He is then the 'free rider' a in Figure 3.1 (p. 46) who, as long as no exchange has taken place, profits from the quantity q^b bought by b without contributing to its cost.

The consequences of the second assumption were examined not by Wicksell, but by Olson. When others will not contribute to the production of the social good, it depends on the shape of his demand curve whether it is worth while for him to produce the social good at his own expense. Most individual demand curves are low in respect of the marginal cost of the social good. If they are just as low as or even lower than the demand curve D^a shown in Figure 3.1 the individual citizen will achieve his own optimum merely by doing nothing. It is only when some individuals, who are in contact with each other, value a good very highly that they will produce it for their own account.

The difference between Marx's assumption and Olson's hypothesis will now also become clear in another respect. If the group or the class (in Marx's model) is homogeneous, *no single* social good will be produced despite the group's interest. After all, there will be no one whose preference for a certain social good is sufficiently intense for him to be prepared to produce it at his own expense. It is only when a group is heterogeneous that some collective actions will be undertaken, even though these will be less in number and quality than would be an optimum for the group as a whole. Furthermore, those whose utility is much improved by these activities will be forced to pay a relatively large share in the costs because of the absence of the others during the negotiations.

The democratic acceptance of coercion

Schmidt and Van der Veen (1976, p. 186) noted that the Prisoners' Dilemma is not a result of a specific outcome matrix but of a certain pay-off matrix. In the examples, the Prisoners' Dilemma is a result of the fact that in all cases the individuals prefer a light to a heavy prison sentence, and a small to a large contribution to the costs. It is obvious that a way out of the Prisoners' Dilemma must be sought by a change in the pay-off matrix.

Olson argues that to ensure a sufficient degree of participation it is in the group's own interest to give selective stimuli to individual group members. In my opinion, these selective stimuli really mean that some of the four outcomes of the outcome matrix *will be affected by sanctions* so that the pay-off matrix will change. These sanctions can be positive or negative. Positive sanctions are rewards given to those who cooperate in achieving a socially desirable result. The rewards are given in the form of *private* goods and in such a way that the cooperative strategy will dominate. To stimulate participation, political parties, trade unions and student organisations, for example, can provide personal services which take the form of advice on rents, legal aid, or student counselling (see Olson, 1971, pp. 132ff).

In reality, however, negative sanctions are more common because they are easier to apply. In general, negative sanctions mean that those who do not join in a cooperative strategy will be punished *individually* so that individuals will prefer to cooperate when they take the possibility of being punished into account. Such punishment can be given by persons outside the group, *but also by the group itself.* In the example of the prisoners, it is possible that a man who turns Queen's evidence will be punished by expulsion from the criminal underworld, but it is also possible that both prisoners will agree (provided they are able to communicate) that if one turns Queen's evidence, retaliatory measures will be taken against him.

If members of a group punish themselves when they do not cooperate, Kafoglis (1962, p. 47) speaks of 'a voluntary acceptance of coercion', but I want to change this to *a democratic acceptance of coercion.* The members of the group themselves then make provisions to escape their Prisoners' Dilemma; they do this democratically (e.g. by majority decisions). Olson (1971, p. 86) mentions the paradox which has frequently been observed in American manufacturing industry: over 90 per cent will not attend meetings or participate in union affairs, yet over 90 per cent will vote to force themselves to belong to the union and make considerable payments to it. Before Olson, Wicksell had already drawn attention to a notable example of a democratic acceptance of coercion, *compulsory taxation.* Using this example, Wicksell illustrated a common paradox: voters who evade

paying taxes as much as possible yet vote for higher taxes for
everyone, including themselves. Their self-interest demands that
they contribute as little as possible, but their collective interest
requires that everyone, without exception, is taxed up to a certain
amount.

Economic welfare without coercion?

The necessity to accept coercion resulting from the Prisoners'
Dilemma has disquieted many social scientists, most of whom are
presumably products of the permissive society. Various authors
have tried to find ways of escaping the dilemma without the use of
force. These ways could be summarised as 'responsible behaviour'.
In this paragraph, I shall discuss three forms of 'responsible
behaviour', viz. responsibility resulting from *liability* within a small
group, responsibility as an expression of *an altruistic morality*, and
responsibility for the *future* of society.

A number of sociologists have noted that responsible behaviour
can be stimulated by *de*concentrating the process of decision-making
into small groups. Schumacher did this in his book, *Small is beautiful*
(1973). From the point of view of economics also, there are several
advantages in deconcentration, of which two will be discussed here.
The first advantage is mentioned by Taylor, who remarks: 'the more
numerous the players, the more likely it is that the problem of the
provision of public goods will take the form of a Prisoners'
Dilemma' (1976, p. 132). Here Taylor follows Olson who predicts
that individuals in small groups will behave like oligopolists and
therefore feel *themselves* liable for the influence their behaviour has on
the result reached by the group, themselves included. The second
advantage of deconcentration is that an existing Prisoners' Dilemma
can be removed without coercion merely because those who do not
join in a cooperative strategy are considered irresponsible by the
others and can thus, for example, be discredited. Social pressure is
only effective if the persons affected are bothered by it and if it is
selective, i.e. it hits only those persons who have chosen an undesirable strategy. Such discrimination can be used only in small groups
(see Van den Doel, 1977, pp. 223–6 for further details).

The responsibility individuals in a small group feel for the collective activities within the group does not extend to what happens
outside the group. This is the other side of the arguments in favour of
deconcentration. A firm that has introduced self-management, just
as a capitalist firm, may use its powers to foul the environment thus

passing on some of its production costs to its neighbours. Residents in old districts, who try to get their district renovated, will throw the weeds from their gardens into gardens in the surrounding districts whose welfare can be profoundly influenced by this 'spring-cleaning'. There is something to be said for not making the unit of decision any larger than is necessary to 'internalise' the external effects of the social goods. A further reduction of scale will again call forth further parasitical behaviour, viz. by the one small group in respect of the other.

This might be the reason why Sen (1974) and Hirsch (1977, pp. 137ff) consider it possible to escape from the Prisoners' Dilemma by responsible behaviour based on *an altruistic morality*. Sen has devised two amendments to the Prisoners' Dilemma (PD), viz. the 'Assurance Game' (AG) and the 'Other Regarding Game' (OR). The preferences based on self-interest, which Sen terms 'PD-preferences', are not changed. Yet, individuals do not behave according to their PD-preferences but according to another payoff matrix, which is determined by a 'moral code of behaviour' (Sen, 1974, p. 62). They behave as if they are guided not only by their own self-interest but also by the interests of others.

The *Assurance Game* (AG) assumes that individuals will behave cooperatively as long as others do the same, and that they will cease to cooperate only when others do the same. Individuals do not behave according to PD-preferences but according to AG-preferences. These can be expressed as follows, using the example of the prisoners: 'I consider one year in prison less objectionable than letting my mate down, provided that my mate thinks the same; however, if my mate is prepared to let me down, I'll repay him in kind.' The pay-off matrix in Table 3.4 shows that there are two points of equilibrium in the Assurance Game: if one player cooperates then the Pareto optimum will be reached; as soon as one player ceases to co-operate, the outcome does not satisfy the Paretian criterion.

TABLE 3.4 *Pay-off matrix on the basis of PD-, AG- and OR-preferences*

Prisoners' Dilemma (PD)	Assurance Game (AG)	Other Regarding Game (OR)
(3;3) → (1;4)	(4;4) ← (1;3)	(4;4) ← (3;2)
↓ ↓	↑ ↓	↑ ↑
(4;1) → (2;2)	(3;1) → (2;2)	(2;3) ← (1;1)

The *Other Regarding Game* (OR) is even more altruistic. It assumes that an individual will always cooperate even when others refuse to cooperate. The individuals then behave in accordance with the OR-preferences, e.g. 'I consider letting down my mate worse than 30 years in prison.' The pay-off matrix shows that in this case the socially desirable outcome is always assured.

The weakness of Sen's analysis is that he does not show how the observance of his moral code can be ensured. He suggests that 'society may evolve traditions by which preferences of the OR-type are praised most, AG-type preferences next, and PD-type preferences least of all' (1974, p. 61). If one of the moralists decides to return to egotism, at least in the Assurance Game, the delicate balance will be disturbed. Yet Sen's models are useful because they clearly reveal the role that morality could perhaps play.

The fact that theories on possible escapes from the Prisoners' Dilemma are realistic only if they are based on the striving after self-interest, was appreciated by Taylor. In his book *Anarchy and cooperation* (1976) he elaborates the dilemma of the prisoners into a *Prisoners' Dilemma Supergame* by treating the game as an infinite number of repeated games, in which each player knows the strategies chosen by the other player in the previous games. It becomes apparent that such a 'supergame' can produce a Paretian optimum equilibrium when two conditions are met, which are interdependent to some extent. The first condition is that the players can choose one of two *conditional strategies*. These are somewhat similar to the strategies in the Assurance Game, but they differ in at least one respect. In these conditional strategies a player only ceases to cooperate when the other player did the same in the *preceding* game. This difference is important but Taylor's most significant contribution lies in his second condition for an optimum. This is the condition by which *both players have an interest in maintaining the cooperation already established*. The cooperative equilibrium is not stable in the Assurance Game because the PD-preferences continue to exist so that each of the two players find it attractive to cease cooperating so that his first PD-priority and not his second PD-priority can be achieved. In the Prisoners' Dilemma *Super*game this is not inevitably the case. The player who ceases to cooperate does, admittedly, gain a short-term advantage. At the same time he loses in the long run: because the other player will follow his bad example, he will achieve not his second but only his third priority in all subsequent games. Now, everything will depend on how the players value their future gains relative to their present gains. If they have a low discount rate, i.e. if they do not value future results much less than present results, it is rational to maintain the cooperation already established. If their discount rate is high, however, then it is rational to cease cooperating.

Without using these self-same words, Taylor has given a new interpretation of *responsible behaviour* which he implicitly regards as behaviour *directed at the personal future*, and which, also when self-interest determines behaviour, guarantees a Paretian optimum equilibrium at least in a two-person game.

The end of 'laissez-faire'

On page 41 I argued that there are two elements in a negotiations democracy: free exit and non-commitment. In a negotiations democracy, none of the individuals is able to force other individuals to participate in the group negotiations or to accept the outcome of negotiations. In the previous paragraphs it has become clear that as long as individuals are not greatly concerned about their own future, there is not much chance of an outcome of the negotiations being reached which satisfies the criterion of Pareto. Such an optimum can be achieved only when individuals *are* able to force each other to contribute to the costs of social goods.

When the members of the group accept these conclusions and decide to apply negative sanctions to those who do not participate or do not contribute, then we can speak of a *democratic acceptance of coercion* (see p. 57). Such an acceptance also means that the basis of a negotiations democracy disappears. A democratic acceptance of coercion does not mean the *end of negotiations but the end of freedom of exit and of non-commitment*. It is the end of 'laissez faire, laissez passer' because it has become clear that, in a large group, during the process of negotiations on the basis of non-commitment, there is no invisible hand which harmonises the self-interest of various people.

Pryor (1968) and Wilensky (1975) have shown how the *growth* of the government in all modern economies can be explained in part by the striving of all individuals after optimum utility. I argue that the existence of a government in all modern economies can partly be explained by the same striving. After all, the members of a large group need an instrument with which they can punish those who do not fulfil their obligations under the agreements reached within the group. One of the instruments considered most suitable is the establishment of a group government which has a monopoly of physical force and which can therefore compel the members of the group to submit to group decisions. This applies not only to state or munici- pal authorities; a group government can also be formed by the executives of a private club.

Taylor (1976, pp. 3, 11, 126–7) has made it clear that this explana- tion of the existence and functioning of a government dates from the political philosophers of the seventeenth and eighteenth centuries, among whom were Hobbes and Hume, and that it can even be found in the writings of the Chinese philosopher Han Fei Tzu who died in 233 B.C. According to Taylor, Hobbes considered individual prefer- ences as a combination of egotism and malevolence, while Hume saw them as a mixture of egotism and benevolence even though egotism dominated. The outcome is the same. By the use of quota- tions, Taylor shows that both in fact described the Prisoners' Dilemma in which the individuals become trapped, that both came to the conclusion that the use of coercion was in the interest of all individuals, and that both inferred the existence of a government. Whereas Hobbes confined himself to the static version of the Prison- ers' Dilemma, Hume also bore in mind the time factor and the negative influence of a high discount rate. Whereas Hobbes explained that the function of a government primarily stems from the need to provide the collective goods 'peace and security', Hume gave a wider definition to the welfare effects of the government: 'bridges are built; harbours open'd; ramparts rais'd; canals form'd; fleets equipp'd; and armies disciplin'd; every where, by the care of government' (Taylor, 1976, p. 126).

3.3 Negotiations democracy in practice

Defence and development cooperation

Wicksell and Olson's theories have received support recently from elementary empirical studies. I have already mentioned the studies (though not based on Olson's theories) by the sociologist Lammers on the decision-making process at Dutch universities. I have also noted that Olson himself published the results of an investigation into the success achieved by the American trade unions in their attempt to introduce closed shops. Three years after the publication of *The logic of collective action*, Olson and Zeckhauser (1968) applied the theory of parasitical behaviour to social goods provided by military and political alliances, especially by NATO. They regard NATO as a collection of member states who have formed a group with freedom of exit and, at least in peace time, without commitment, in order to supply a social good (the building-up of a defensive apparatus capable of deterring a potential aggressor). They distinguish between the two categories of goods making up this defensive apparatus, the troops and the infrastructure.

Decisions of the alliance in respect of the troops are the result of multilateral negotiations. Large countries have more inhabitants, a higher national income and have traditionally had bigger armies. Smaller countries, which have always had to be content with small armies, according to the theory, will be inclined to shelter under the military umbrella of the large countries, thus behaving as a 'free rider'. If they have social-democratic governments they will motivate this type of behaviour by a neutral or pacifist ideology. Next, Olson and Zeckhauser test this hypothesis against the facts which show that the large countries do in fact contribute considerably more to NATO forces than is commensurate with the size of their national income.

In respect of the infrastructure (bases, depots), NATO decisions on construction and division of the costs are the result of bilateral negotiations. In theory there is little opportunity here for parasitical behaviour and indeed the facts show that it does not occur. On the contrary, the smaller countries which benefit most in economic terms from the infrastructure, contribute more to the costs than is commensurate with the size of their national income.

Thoben (1971) tried to reach the same conclusion in respect of the policy of international aid and development. The provision of development aid by rich countries to poor countries can be seen as a social good in so far as it contributes to the stability of world peace and a quiet social conscience of the rich. This social good can be provided multilaterally (via international organisations) or bilaterally (via separate agreements between a rich and a poor country). In the latter case, selective benefits can be attached to the rich countries with regard to exports. Thoben noted that the total amount of multilateral aid is considerably smaller than bilateral aid and according to him, this corroborates the hypothesis that multilateral negotiations without selective stimuli lead to a result which is less than an optimum even for the rich countries. On the distribution of costs, however, he got no further than the supposition that larger countries would contribute more than proportionally, and the smaller countries less than proportionally, to total multilateral aid. This disproportion would be somewhat compensated by bilateral aid. In my opinion it is possible to interpret Thoben's conclusions thus: as long as there is no authoritative world government, bilateral negotiations between the countries involved lead to a better result for all concerned than do multilateral negotiations.

Burgess and Robinson (1969) tried to test Olson's theory using a 'man-machine' simulation in which 150 players were divided into a number of decision-making teams representing nations. At the beginning of the game there were two types of coalitions between the nations, viz. one type that only provided social goods to the coalition partners (in the form of peace, security and economic power) and another type that combined the provision of social goods with the selective granting of private benefits (private goods in the form of funds for domestic projects) to the separate coalition partners. Both investigators measured the effectiveness of both types of coalition by questioning the players after some time had elapsed (i.e. when many decisions had been taken) about the general effectiveness of the coalition, the likelihood that the coalition would succeed in maintaining peace, and the contribution of the coalition in attaining domestic goals. They concluded that the second type of coalition was much more effective than the first type, and that a large degree of this effectiveness was due to the supplementary provision of private goods. Their study is a useful application of simulation techniques for testing decision-making theories.

Full employment and the social contract

In the last two subsections of this chapter an empirical example of negotiations democracy in practice is discussed; this example has been analysed extensively elsewhere by Van den Doel, De Galan and Tinbergen (1976). It deals with the provision of full employment by means of a 'central accord' or a 'social contract'. In 1973 in the Netherlands the cabinet led by Den Uyl, in which the social democrats dominated, attempted to persuade the trade unions to lower the rate of growth of wages by means of a 'central accord' in which the employers and employees reach an agreement on the basis of a certain government policy. Since 1974, the Labour cabinets in England led by Wilson and Callaghan, have attempted to do the same, using a 'social contract'. On the basis of Wicksell's and Olson's theories, Van den Doel, De Galan and Tinbergen concluded that even if central accords and social contracts were signed, they would provide insufficient scope for an effective employment policy, so that the macro-economic aims formulated by the employees themselves cannot be achieved in this way. The three authors discussed only the type of unemployment resulting from a shortage of capital. Such unemployment must be *combated* with extra investments in either the private or the public sector of the economy. As the employees have announced that they want to maintain the existing level of transfer incomes, the extra investments will have to be financed to a large extent by reducing the rate of growth of incomes. But the three authors feel that, in an economy in which wage negotiations are based on freedom of exit and non-commitment, such a reduction will not be realised sufficiently.

Up to the present this conclusion has been borne out by the facts. Neither the British nor the Dutch social-democratic governments succeeded even once in achieving a social contract or a central accord. In England the voluntary restraint of the TUC led in the years 1975, 1976 and 1977 to a fall in the rate of increase in nominal wages; this increase was 30, 20 and 7 per cent respectively, while the government had set a limit varying between 5 and 10 per cent. But the TUC self-restraint, brought about by a 'crisis' atmosphere, was only temporary in nature. At the end of 1977 the trade unions announced that they would not cooperate further, so that the British government found it necessary to attempt coercion by 'punishing' firms which paid more than 10 per cent wage increases. In the Netherlands, the trade unions also agreed voluntarily to lower wage increases. Despite this the average nominal increase in wages in the period 1974–76 was 13 per cent per year although the government had set an (initial) limit of 8 per cent. Van den Doel, De Galan and Tinbergen see the cause of the failure to lower wage increases on the basis of 'concerted action' (viz. without coercion) as a result of the fact that the trade unions and employers' organisations have no power to settle the conflicts of interest in the economy. As a result the separate groups and individuals who belong to the trade unions and the employers' organisations are caught up in a large-scale Prisoners' Dilemma (see also Ellman, 1966, p. 249; Hirsch, 1977, p. 145).

Assume, purely for argument's sake, that all workers and employers strive after an active and effective employment policy as a *social* good. However, they hold different opinions on the distribution of income: each individual strives after a change in the distribution in his own favour. In Table 3.5 the goals in the fields of employment and income distribution are combined. It appears (in

TABLE 3.5 *Hypothetical ordering of preferences by an individual*

Priority no.	Does the individual pay for employment himself?	Do others pay for the employment?	What is the effect on the relative income position of the individual?	Does employment recover?
1	No	Yes	Better	Yes
2	Yes	Yes	Unchanged	Yes
3	No	No	Unchanged	No
4	Yes	No	Worse	No

the example) every individual worker and employer arranged his preferences as follows:

(1) his highest priority is to create employment at another's expense; this will improve his relative income position and employment will recover;

(2) his second priority is to create employment at everyone's (including his own) expense; this means his relative income position will be unchanged and employment will recover;

(3) his third priority is that no employment is created so that no one (including himself) need pay anything; his relative income thus remains unchanged, but employment does not recover;

(4) his lowest priority is when employment is created but he alone pays for it while others sponge on his generosity; this worsens his relative income position, but because a sacrifice by a single individual is as a drop in the ocean, employment does not recover.

In a political democracy in which binding decisions can be taken, the eventual choice will concentrate on the real alternatives 2 (everyone shares in the costs) or 3 (nobody pays). The parasitical alternatives 1 and 4, in which some share in the costs and others do not, may be excluded in principle. In the example, the individuals will vote for priority 2 so that employment will recover. But in the world of trade unions and employers' organisations, which are not able to take binding decisions, all four alternatives are possible. An individual worker or employer is uncertain about the decision of the others. As long as he cannot bind the other workers and employers (i.e. punish them with negative sanctions) he will be afraid that as soon as he has decided to make a sacrifice in order to improve employment, he will have chosen priority 4 which means that the others will not share in the costs so that his relative income position will worsen without his achieving the desired result in increased employment. So long as the other employers and workers are unable to bind him by their vote (i.e. to punish him by applying sanctions) he will be tempted to choose his highest priority by which others will pay for the creation of employment so that his relative income position will improve. The fact that the decision-making process is unable to bind the participants means that the individual is caught up in a dilemma: he does want employment to be created, but out of the desire to avoid payment and the fear that others will succeed in doing the same, he will refrain from contributing. As all individual workers and employers argue this way, no one will make a sacrifice. In a referendum democracy or a representative democracy (assuming that politicians have the power to forbid the parasitic alternatives), the second priority will be chosen and implemented. But in trade unions and employers' organisations, which cannot do much more than hold discussions which commit no one, the third and not the first or second priority will be chosen. In this model, the employers' aims of combating unemployment will never be realised.

The authors argue that there are at least two possible ways of escaping from this Prisoners' Dilemma. The common element in these possibilities can be found in *giving workers the power to apply sanctions* against those who support both full employment and the greater equality of incomes but try to evade contributing to the costs.

The first method is for the government to apply sanctions on behalf of the workers. This is the method of a central incomes policy. After detailed negotiations with trade unions and employers' organisations, the workers' representatives in parliament will take the final decision on wages and other incomes and will instruct the cabinet to ensure that everyone, or nearly everyone, contributes to the costs of an effective employment policy. In the terminology of the Prisoners' Dilemma, this means that the government will exclude the parasitic alternatives 1 and 4 and let the majority choose between the real alternatives 2 and 3.

The authors point out that the majority will only voluntarily accept such a coercion if three conditions are met:

(1) In the workers' individual objective functions social goods and (macro-economic) aims, which can be realised only by collective action, carry a large weight.
(2) The workers believe that the government (the cabinet and parliament) are able to realise these aims.

(3) The workers do not regard government as the instrument of a 'hostile' group, but as an instrument of the workers themselves which can be used to divide the benefits and costs fairly.

However, there is also a second method of escape from the Prisoners' Dilemma. In this second way, power is given to the trade unions and not to the government to take binding decisions on wages, prices and social goods. Van den Doel, De Galan and Tinbergen have summarised this method in three behavioural rules (contra Olson, 1971, p. 44 n. 66). Firstly, the government will force the trade unions' hand by presenting them with a number of alternatives in which the public sector, differing in size and composition, is combined with the corresponding wage increase (e.g. three alternatives in which the incidence of taxes and social insurance will increase by 1.0 per cent, 0.5 per cent and 0.0 per cent of the national income and in which *real* negotiated wages will rise by −1.0 per cent, +1.0 per cent and +3.0 per cent respectively). Secondly, the trade unions organise a referendum among all their members. Thirdly, both the government and the trade unions announce beforehand that they will consider the result of the referendum as committing them, i.e. binding them in respect of the size of the public sector and the level of real wages. This method is a step in the direction of a *corporate state*.

The choice between the first and second method cannot be based on the criterion of Pareto, but depends, among other things, on the relative power one wishes to accord to the members of the trade unions and to other voters.

A discussion on the 'democratic acceptance of coercion'

The conclusion that a reduction in wage increase cannot be achieved by negotiations which commit none of the parties – employers, workers and the government – but that it can be achieved if there is a democratic acceptance of coercion, led to a lively discussion in the Netherlands not only among economists but also among sociologists, politicians and trade union leaders; leading articles also appeared in the newspapers and the weeklies. Public opinion surveys (e.g. NIPO, 22 March 1976) showed that about 40 per cent of the Dutch people (and likewise 40 per cent of Dutch trade union members) agreed with the three authors and about 60 per cent disagreed. Yet the comments of those who joined in the public discussion were nearly always negative.

The summary below gives the most important objections of the opponents on the left-hand side; these have been classified into four groups for the sake of convenience. The brief answers to these objections are given on the right-hand side.

Objection	Answer
1. The assumptions in the model are unrealistic.	*A model is nothing more than an idealisation of a real situation. The question, however, is whether the assumptions are so lacking in actuality that the conclusions have to be rejected.*
1a. The workers do not strive only after their own self-interest but also after the interests of others.	The workers will choose a (socially desirable) cooperative strategy only if they place a higher value on the interests of others than on their own self-interest (as Sen simulated in his 'Other Regarding Game'). However, I do not consider such an assumption to be realistic. As long as even the socialist republics of Russia, China and Cuba have not succeeded in creating a new, socialist human being, I cannot see how this can be achieved in a mixed economic order.
1b. The workers are not as stupid as the three authors assume, and will therefore voluntarily reduce their wage increases.	It is an error to think that the Prisoners' Dilemma assumes that the workers are stupid. If the theory of games has a single weakness it is that it assumes the exact opposite – that the workers are intelligent. Stupid, foolish workers will lower their demands because the Prime Minister, or the author of this book, says so. But it is precisely the intelligent workers who calmly survey the battle field, calculate their chances, and then fall into the trap of the Prisoners' Dilemma.
1c. It is not legitimate to jump from a simple model like the Prisoners' Dilemma to policy conclusions.	The authors have placed three strict conditions on the application of the model to economic policy (see pp. 67, 68). One of them holds that the workers believe an incomes policy will be effectitive in realising their own (collective) aims.

Objection	Answer
2. The Prisoners' Dilemma can be removed without coercion.	In general, these objections are based on an incomplete insight into the application of the Prisoners' Dilemma Game to the provision of social goods in a large group.
2a. The Prisoners' Dilemma can be removed by improving the communication between the two prisoners. If they are not isolated, they can agree on a cooperative strategy.	This argument is valid only for a small group, in which the members of the group will take into account the effects of their own decisions on the whole group. In a large group the individuals will assume that their individual decisions will have no influence on the total result, and good communication will confirm the validity of this assumption.
2b. The Prisoners' Dilemma can be removed when the government, as soon as it becomes evident that voluntary reduction is not successful, punishes the workers collectively by freezing social security payments and lowering the level of public expenditure.	An overt threat to punish collectively will only enable the workers to escape the Prisoners' Dilemma when it is combined with a binding referendum among trade unionists (see p. 68). If such a referendum is either not held or not binding, each trade unionist will assume that his individual decision to lower the rise of his income will not influence the possibility that the punishment will indeed be meted out so that the Prisoners' Dilemma continues to exist.
3. Even under coercion the Prisoners' Dilemma cannot be removed.	This argument has been disproved time and again, both in literature and in history.
3a. Not only trade unions but also political parties are caught up in the Prisoners' Dilemma. Shifting the level of decision-making from the trade unions to parliament would therefore solve nothing.	In my opinion, this argument has been sufficiently refuted (see pp. 57, 58). A government can apply sanctions to voters who do not meet their payment obligations (seizure, fines, imprisonment). A trade union cannot apply these sanctions. Assume that the voters prefer the universal lowering of individual wage increases (priority 2 in Table 3.5) to a complete lack of wage restraint (priority 3). If the members

of a trade union must decide on a future reduction in wage increases the workers, as trade unionists, decide against a reduction because no sanctions can be taken against those individuals (both within and without the trade unions) who will wish to evade the measures. If the voters must decide on this moderation, the same workers, *as citizens*, will vote for political parties who support moderation by everyone and of which (on the basis of their policy in the past) it can be expected that they will enforce it by government measures. So, the question is not whether trade unions or political parties are caught up in a Prisoners' Dilemma, but that individuals are caught up in it as trade unionists but not as voters.

3b. A central incomes policy cannot be carried out because coercion has little effect if it is applied against the will of those concerned.

The three authors have assumed that a central incomes policy is the result of a *democratic* acceptance of coercion (e.g. by parliamentary elections). The use of coercion is thus democratically legitimised. The argument that coercion is not effective has often been used in the past but has seldom proved correct. In spite of the supposed ineffectiveness of democratically accepted coercion, the voters in all Atlantic economies are at present paying, under coercion, between 30 and 50 per cent of the national income in taxes and social insurance contributions.

4. The democratic acceptance of coercion arouses important political objections.

There is always a possibility, that political objections will be raised to the outcome of the model. After all, in my opinion, no normative validity can be attributed to a Paretian optimum (p. 37), so that each person is entitled to discard the conclusions of welfare economics on moral or social grounds.

Objection	*Answer*
	However, when the 'political objections' are based on misunderstandings, then they can be removed.
4*a*. The authors speak of an incomes policy, but they mean only a wage policy.	Two of the three authors (Tinbergen and De Galan) have for many years been closely engaged in designing a general incomes policy concerning all incomes and they have frequently proposed a far-reaching income–equalisation (see, for example, Tinbergen, 1975, 1976).
4*b*. An incomes policy always degenerates into a wage policy only.	The authors have stressed that an incomes policy can only be accepted democratically if it is implemented by politicians, who are seen by the workers as their representatives. In that case, the danger of an incomes policy 'degenerating' is not very realistic.
4*c*. A wages and incomes policy excludes the workers from participating in wage determination.	The workers *are not being excluded in a way that they are at present excluded*. Now the workers do not have the policy instruments to realise their own wishes in respect of social goods. By way of an incomes policy the workers are given the weapons they need to enforce the implementation of their own majority decisions.

4

Majority decision

4.1 Majority and utility

The economic policy optimum theorem

In this chapter I shall discuss referendum democracy, which I take to be a decision-making model in which the group members take *binding* collective decisions without the intervention of representatives. This type of direct democracy seldom occurs as an independent model. The examples discussed in this chapter are, curiously enough, derived from other models of decision-making, in particular from representative democracy. However, a discussion of referendum democracy is necessary because a referendum democracy in its abstract form has three elements which are to be found in most other decision-making models. The first element is that the group has a government which can ensure that all group decisions will be observed by all members of the group so that the elements of 'freedom of exit' and 'non-commitment', which had a central position in a negotiations democracy, have been eliminated here. The second element is that this group government not only ensures that unanimous decisions taken by all group members will be carried out but also that *majority decisions* will be observed by a minority. The third element is that both this majority and this minority can consist of individuals with different objective functions.

The arrangement of this chapter is as follows. In the first part binding majority decisions will be discussed from the viewpoint of utility. The second part will examine the question whether majority decisions can be consistent, while in the final part an analysis is given of some effects of majority decisions on welfare.

The chapter thus begins with a few remarks on (binding) majority decisions from the viewpoint of utility. Wicksell (Musgrave and Peacock, 1967, pp. 87ff) formulated his famous unanimity rule in 1886, which states that all decisions about public goods and the concomitant division of costs must be unanimous, to prevent an individual from being exploited by others. In an essay devoted to this fundamental rule, Hennipman (1977, pp. 231–53) indicated the unanimity rule by the term *economic policy optimum theorem*, to emphasise that the unanimity rule is based on a philosophy which can be regarded as the counterpart of the Paretian economic optimum theorem. This philosophy, like that of Pareto, thinks in terms of achieving 'utopian efficiency' – which is done by framing rules which, in a utopian world, would ensure that problems such as the distribution of incomes would be satisfactorily solved so that a situation of maximum utility could be attained. More precisely, the unanimity rule in a utopian society is a method of ensuring that political decisions satisfy the Paretian criterion. Conversely, the existence of unanimity proves empirically that the Paretian criterion has been met. When, initially, there is no unanimity, an attempt can be made to achieve it by compensating the losers so that they will then agree to the proposed changes.

However, in a non-utopian society the situation is different. Then unanimity should not be regarded as proof of the existence of a Paretian optimum. Nor is the lack of unanimity proof that a Paretian optimum has *not* been achieved. In the essay already mentioned, Hennipman points out that in fact it is not true that all individuals prefer a Paretian optimum to a situation which is not a Pareto optimum, not even when the losers are completely compensated. Paretian improvements can, for example, have as their result that utility can increase very unequally. It is possible that those individuals whose utility decreases in relative terms will vote against a change despite the fact that their utility increases in absolute terms. More generally, I have already pointed out (see pp. 36–7) that no normative validity can be attributed to a Paretian optimum. Individuals will always test a Paretian improvement against their ultimate (ethical) norms, e.g. in respect of income distribution. Many individuals will generally prefer a non-Pareto optimum with an equitable distribution to a Paretian optimum with an inequitable distribution.

Yet, unanimity is not ensured even when the increase in utility conforms both to the Paretian criterion and to the individuals' ethical norms. It is possible that the individuals are insufficiently informed about the costs and benefits of a specific project and therefore are wrong in turning it down. Furthermore, in a situation in which decisions must be unanimous, each individual is in a too powerful negotiating position. By threatening to veto every group decision he can, when he plays his cards aright, make the others carry a disproportionate share of the costs (Buchanan, 1968, pp. 92–7). The outcome of this type of multilateral negotiation, which is the result of strategic behaviour, is indeterminate.

A simple or a qualified majority?

The economic policy optimum theorem thus only has, as for example has the norm of perfect competition, meaning as an ideal. It is totally useless as a practical norm. Wicksell recognised this when he diluted the condition of unanimity 'for practical purposes' to a qualified majority of, for example, 75 per cent or 90 per cent, which he called 'relative unanimity'. The question arises whether it would not have been 'more practical' to lower this percentage further to, let us say, 51 per cent. The higher the percentage, the more the Scylla threatens that small groups will exploit their power, thus transforming the process of negotiation to a Polish Diet or an Indonesian Musjawarah. The lower the percentage, the closer one comes to the Charybdis where the majority will appropriate all the benefits of the public goods and will charge the minority with the payment of the costs.

In *The Calculus of Consent* (1965, pp. 63–84) Buchanan and Tullock indicated how both dangers can best be avoided. The graph in Figure 4.1 shows their solution. The horizontal axis gives the decision rule, i.e. the percentage (of group members) whose approval is required for a specific group decision to be taken. The vertical axis shows the overall costs for each individual with this decision rule. Buchanan and Tullock have subdivided these costs in two categories: external costs and decision-making costs.

The *external costs* (curve E) arise because of the utility costs to the losers. External costs thus come about because the group forces an individual to contribute to collective actions which he considers undesirable (at that price). Seen from the viewpoint of this individual, external costs are the result of wrong decisions. They equal the loss in utility resulting from these wrong decisions. The higher the percentage required for a group decision, the lower the chance of wrong decisions being taken so that curve E falls.

Decision-making costs (curve B) are the costs valued in money of the time and energy an individual invests in the process of negotiation. The greater the requirement for unanimity the higher the decision-making costs, partly because it becomes increasingly profitable for some individuals to behave strategically. Curve B therefore rises.

Figure 4.1 *The choice of the decision rule by an individual*

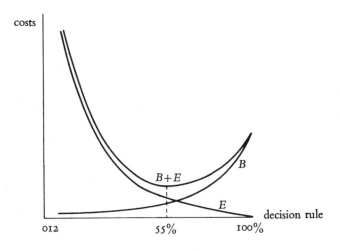

Source: Bish, 1971, p. 40

Buchanan and Tullock hold that each individual will choose the decision rule which minimises the sum of both categories of costs. In the example given in Figure 4.1 this point is where a majority of 55 per cent of the votes is required for a group decision.

Even though it is difficult to determine the shape of the B and E curves empirically, it is possible to draw a number of logical conclusions from Buchanan and Tullock's model. It is clear that in this model the well-known 'majority rule' with which decisions are taken by the half plus one is just as arbitrary as every other decision rule. There is no reason to prefer 51 per cent to 49 per cent unless it can be shown that the total cost curve is always at a minimum at 51 per cent.

The optimum decision rule varies with the type of collective decision. In the case of constituent decisions, i.e. decisions on decision rules (revisions to the constitution), the external cost curve will rise sharply so that the minimum of the total cost curve moves to the right. The individuals desire relative unanimity in such a case and accept the concomitant higher decision-making costs. After all, a faulty constitution has continuing consequences and their effects are unpredictable: today's dictator is often tomorrow's victim of his own laws. However, if the decisions are allocative, i.e. decisions on collective actions on the basis of given decision rules, then the *E* curve will be considerably less sharp, so that the minimum of the total cost curve moves to the left. Most individuals will then prefer a decision rule involving small decision costs, for example a simple majority. In this case the costs and benefits are once-only and their size is to some extent predictable.

Buchanan and Tullock thus present a paradoxical situation in which an optimum is reached in the utility of all individuals when the possibility of realising a Paretian optimum is discarded. For the decision-making costs of reaching a Paretian optimum are prohibitive.

The iron law of oligarchy

In my opinion Buchanan and Tullock's model sheds light on *das eherne Gesetz der Oligarchie* (the iron law of oligarchy) formulated by the sociologist Robert Michels (1911; 1962). He sketches an inevitable process of the decline of every democracy, the process of conversion to oligarchy. A small, independent, complacent group of political leaders, on the crest of the wave of a democratic movement, will always succeed in imposing its will on the masses. Michels gave a sociological interpretation of this process (he dealt with representative, not direct, democracy) and his witness for the prosecution was social-democracy. His explanatory model has two supports: the need to organise, and the growing independence of political leadership. J. J. A. Van Doorn (1969, pp. 17–18) has simplified his theory to a 'quasi-syllogism':
– *democracy* means *the influence of the masses*;
– *the influence of the masses* implies *organisation*: the masses unite and show their fist;
– *organisation* necessitates *leadership*: the fist must deliver an accurate blow;
– *leadership* implies the *subordination* of those led;
– *subordination* of the masses to a group of leaders is termed *oligarchy*;
  thus: democracy leads to oligarchy, not because of a fatal coincidence or malicious design, but because of an inherent law.
It is possible, in my opinion, to reach the same conclusion in respect of direct, not representative, democracy. This is done by using *economic* arguments. The economic analogy of Michels' law is based, for the sake of simplicity, on only one assumption: the desire of all individuals to avoid the high costs of decision-making. The

essence of the economic approach can also be simplied to a 'quasi-syllogism':

- *direct democracy* is worth while, in the eyes of its protagonists, only in the case of *mass participation*;
- *participation by the masses* results in high *costs of decision-making* for each participating individual (see p. 75);
- these *costs of decision-making* are so high that all individuals accept decision rules by which the decisions are taken by a *minority*;
- this *minority* is always composed of the *same* group of persons, viz. those individuals who strive after political power or who value public goods so highly that their individual benefits exceed the costs even when they pay nearly all the costs of participation themselves (see p. 56).
- the taking of decisions by a *permanent minority* is termed *oligarchy*;

thus: participation by the masses results (in a direct democracy) in oligarchy, not because the 'leaders' seize power, but because of the voluntary abdication of the masses.

4.2 Majority and rationality

The macro-political paradox

In Chapter 2, I based my argument on the assumption that all individuals in a group decide consistently, which means that they can compare the policy alternatives with each other (requirement of connectedness) and that they can arrange them in a fixed order (requirement of transitivity). But the eighteenth-century philosopher Condorcet, the nineteenth-century mathematician C. L. Dodgson (alias Lewis Carroll), the twentieth-century economist K. J. Arrow (1951) and the econometrician Duncan Black (1958) have shown that the mere fact that the individuals in a group strive after a consistent goal does not necessarily mean that the group also has a consistent goal. In certain circumstances it is possible that when the individual preferences are added by means of voting, the preference ordering of the group as a whole becomes intransitive. This phenomenon can be termed a *macro-political paradox* by analogy to Keynes' macro-economic paradox which may occur whenever the preferences of individuals are added by the market. When the macro-political paradox occurs, it becomes impossible to form a stable majority. This can be illustrated by means of a not unrealistic example, which is derived not from referendum democracy but from representative democracy.

Let us assume that a parliament is divided into three political groups: right, centre-left, and radical left, and that none of these groups has an absolute majority. Assume also that right and centre-left prefer a moderate to a radical socialist as prime minister, that centre-left and radical left prefer a radical socialist to a convinced conservative as prime minister, and finally, that the right *and the radical left* prefer a convinced conservative to a moderate socialist as prime minister. The collective preference ordering is then intransitive, even though the individual preferences of right, centre-left and the radical left are consistent. This type of collective intransitivity can lead to a state of affairs such as existed during the Fourth Republic in France (1946–59): there were continuous cabinet crises, governments succeeded each other rapidly, each party had a turn at providing the prime minister, and private citizens lost their faith in democracy as a method of coordinating decisions.

Pen tries to find the cause of this collective intransitivity in the preference ordering of the left: in the example a relatively extreme prime minister (convinced conservative or radical socialist) is preferred by the radical left to a relatively moderate prime minister. He concludes: 'This paradox shows that extremists do democracy even more disservices than the obvious ones' (Pen, 1966, pp. 190–1, n.). The significance of this conclusion will be discussed in the next subsection.

Using mathematical symbols Arrow (1951; 1963, pp. 24–31 and 96–103) showed that, if the method of summation of individual preferences *satisfies five apparently reasonable conditions*, it is impossible to assure that the group's decisions will not be paradoxical. Basing myself in part on Riker and Ordeshook (1973, pp. 86–92) and Rowley and Peacock (1975, pp. 36–8) I shall give Arrow's conditions of fairness in my own words:

(1) The individual's freedom of choice must not be restricted. All possible individual preference orderings must be admissible.

(2) The voting procedure must be such that a 'Paretian' relationship exists between the preferences of the individual members of the group and the group as a whole; for example, if the group prefers X to Y, and if for some individuals the preference of X in respect of Y becomes greater without becoming smaller for other individuals, then the group will continue to prefer X to Y.

(3) The result of a vote between two alternatives must depend solely on the preference orderings the individuals have in respect of both these alternatives. (In the third section of this chapter it will

be seen that this condition is met if there is one alternative which in an imaginary series of contests always gets a majority.)

(4) The group is sovereign and need not heed a 'public purpose' which people outside the group try to impose on it.

(5) Within the group there is no dictatorship; the outcome of the group's vote is determined by more than one individual.

Arrow's theorem, the literal formulation and the proof of which are outside the scope of this book, has the following purport: when, in order to add individual preferences, a method is applied which meets each of the conditions 1, 2, 3, 4, and 5, collective transitivity is not ensured. In other words: *if the voting procedure is fair, the result can be paradoxical.*

Extremism and democracy

Black (1958; 1971, pp. 14–25) tried to formulate the conditions to be met if collective transitivity is certain to be ensured. The gist of his conclusion is that the collective preference ordering will always be transitive if all individual preference orderings can be represented as a set of single-peaked curves. To understand what Black means I shall briefly explain his method of graphic representation of individual preference orderings.

In Figure 4.2 the horizontal axes show three policy alternatives a, b and c, and the vertical axes show the individuals' preference order 1, 2 and 3 which individuals can have. The distance between 1, 2 and 3 has no meaning since the scale is purely ordinal. Assume that A's preferences are: $b > a > c$. A's preference ordering is thus single-peaked as the left-hand side of Figure 4.2 shows. From the most-preferred alternative b, the lines to both the left and the right fall. B's preference ordering ($a > b > c$) is also single-peaked. But C's preference ordering ($a > c > b$) is nonsingle-peaked as the right half of Figure 4.2 shows. However, it would be wrong now to draw the conclusion that C is the spoil-sport who prefers the two extreme alternatives to the moderate alternative. In this case the fact that it is precisely C whose preference is nonsingle-peaked is purely fortuitous; I just happened to put a to the left, b in the middle and c to the right. In another sequence C's curve would not only be single-peaked, but A or B's curves might be nonsingle-peaked. (This argument somewhat modifies Pen's criticism of 'extremism'.)

Black holds that it is essential that at least one sequence is found where none of the curves is nonsingle-peaked. More precisely his theorem states: when a set of individual preference orderings can be

Figure 4.2 *Single-peaked and nonsingle-peaked orders of preference*

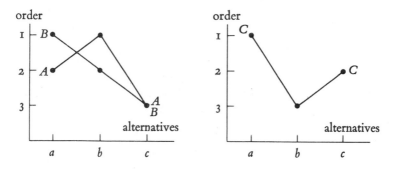

represented graphically *by an appropriate arrangement of the alternatives on the x-axis* as a set of single-peaked curves only, then the collective preference ordering is transitive and there will be one alternative which in a contest with the other alternatives always gets a majority. For example, in Figure 4.2 the collective preference ordering is transitive because all curves will be single-peaked if alternative *a* is placed in the middle. There is thus one alternative which is always chosen by a majority: *B* and *C* prefer *a* to *b* and *a* to *c*, and *A* cannot change this order.

Later studies show that Black has given a sufficient but not a necessary condition for collective transitivity. Sen (1970, pp. 167–86) attempted to formulate the necessary and sufficient condition using, *inter alia*, the concept of 'value-restrictedness'. The 'value' of an alternative is its rank on the *x*-axis. In the example discussed the value of an alternative is thus 1, 2 or 3. A set of individual preference orderings is then value-restricted when all agree that some alternative is not best, or all agree that some alternative is not worst, or all agree that some alternative is not medium. The set of preference orderings in Figure 4.2 (which consists of the preference orderings of *A*, *B* and *C*) is value-restricted in two respects: nowhere does alternative *a* get the value 3, nor does alternative *c* at any time get the value 1.

As Arrow (1963, p. 80) already appreciated, conclusions such as those by Black and Sen provide an insight into the significance of the political culture for a democracy. Political culture is the set of norms, values and goals of a society. Riker and Ordeshook (1973, pp. 104–6) argue that political culture serves to make working of the majority rule possible. Single-peakedness of all preference orderings means that there is a cultural agreement about the criteria on the basis of

which a decision must be taken even though there may be disagreement about the decision itself. For example, all voters vote for the
party which approximates their own opinions most closely; nobody
votes for a party which is furthest removed from his views. Value-
restrictedness means among other things that some alternatives,
even though they are being discussed, are ranked by no one as the
best. For instance: force is only accepted as the last resort. Both
single-peakedness and value-restrictedness mirror a cultural concen-
sus without which democracy cannot function.

The fiscal debate: an empirical example

Lijphart (1975, p. 188) complained that even though the literature
reflects a virtually unanimous opinion on the fact that the macro-
political paradox must occur reasonably often, empirical examples
are almost entirely lacking. Exceptions can be found in one of Riker's
books in which he gives two situations in the American Congress
where the paradox could be seen clearly (Riker and Ordeshook,
1973, p. 99 n. 15), in a small book by Farquharson (1969, pp. 52–3)
who gives a third example from the American Congress, and in an
article by Blydenburgh (1971, pp. 57–71) who again adds two
examples of voting in Congress.

As all these examples are taken from the American Congress, I
shall give an empirical example of the occurrence of the paradox in
one of the European parliaments, the Dutch 'Second Chamber'
which can be compared constitutionally with the House of Com-
mons or the House of Representatives. This example* is taken from
a debate on the excise duty on petrol which took place on the last
night of my membership of the Dutch parliament (28 June 1973).
The debate was about an increase in the excise duty on petrol and
diesel oil. The newly-formed progressive government considered
this increase necessary because it needed the proceeds to finance extra
expenditure. Three alternatives were debated: an increase in duty of
4.5 cents per litre of petrol, of 1.5 cents per litre or of 0.0 cents per
litre.

It was a complicated puzzle to discover the paradox in the *Han-
delingen Tweede Kamer* (Dutch 'Hansard', 1972–73 pp. 2165–2263).
The contents of the speeches had to be interpreted against the back-
ground of the general political line taken by the parties' spokesmen

---

* In Van den Doel (1975a) and Van den Doel (1975b, pp. 82–5) I gave another
example, dealing with a fiscal debate held between 24 November and 1 December
1970.

of the day. It became necessary to interview witnesses and to delve into my own memory. It was inevitably necessary not only to examine the statements of voting intentions but also the actual voting behaviour, the latter not only on 28 June but also on 27 November 1973, because this was when the Budget debate took place and it was when a final decision could be taken. Taking into account the risks inherent in such a method the conclusion is as follows.

During the debate four groups were formed in Parliament, viz.
(1) Socialists (PvdA), radical liberals (D'66), ecologists (PPR), and progressive Protestants (ARP);
(2) Roman Catholics (KVP);
(3) Conservative liberals (VVD, DS'70) and conservative Protestants (CHU);
(4) Communists (CPN) and Pacifists (PSP).

Each of the four groups had a different preference ordering. The Progressives preferred 4.5 cents to 1.5 cents and 1.5 cents to 0.0 cent. The Roman Catholics preferred 1.5 cents to 0.0 cent and 0.0 cent to 4.5 cents. Both the Conservatives and the Communists preferred 0.0 cent. However, the Conservatives put 1.5 cents in the second place and 4.5 cents last, whereas the Communists reversed this order (see Table 4.1).

TABLE 4.1 *Pattern of preferences during the debate on excise duty on petrol* (price increase in cents per litre)

	First choice	Second choice	Third choice	Members present
Progressives	4.5	1.5	0.0	63
Roman Catholics	1.5	0.0	4.5	24
Conservatives	0.0	1.5	4.5	42
Communists	0.0	4.5	1.5	7

Those who favoured majority rule obviously assumed that a majority decision would result in the median, i.e. about 2 cents (Black, 1971, p. 18; Buchanan and Tullock, 1965, p. 136). The actual outcome was 0.0 cent on 28 June however, and 4.5 cents on 27 November 1973. At first a majority was formed (by the Progressives and the Communists) against the 1.5 cents proposed by amendment and when this had been rejected, the Conservatives, Roman

Catholics, and Communists formed a majority for 0.0 cent to the Government's proposal of 4.5 cents. On 28 June there had already been a potential majority (Progressives plus Roman Catholics) who would have preferred 1.5 cents to 0.0 cent, and after that there was to be another majority (Progressives plus Communists) who would have preferred 4.5 cents to 1.5 cents. But the Rules of the Dutch Parliament provide that votes must first be taken on amendments before the Bill itself is considered and also precludes defeated amendments from being voted on again; the potential majority which was present on 28 June could only make itself felt on 27 November when an increase in excise duty of over 4 cents was approved. I had predicted this outcome two months earlier in a scientific analysis of this paradox (Van den Doel, 1973, p. 18 n. 82).

Figure 4.3 shows this voting paradox graphically and illustrates the intransitivity. The x-axis gives the policy alternatives and the y-axis the order of preferences. The set of preference orderings is nonsingle-peaked because the Communists preferred both extremes to the alternative in the middle. Another order of preferences would have laid the cause of the nonsingle-peakedness with the Roman Catholics (RC), the Conservatives or Progressives. The set is not value-restricted because each alternative has the value 1, 2 or 3 in at least one of the preference orderings.

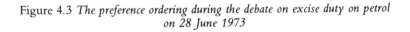

Figure 4.3 *The preference ordering during the debate on excise duty on petrol on 28 June 1973*

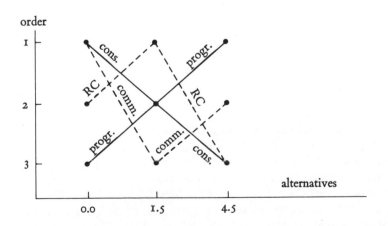

4.3 Majority and economic welfare
Passionate minorities

An important part of the welfare literature on majority decisions consists of discussions on the question of which criteria a voting system must satisfy from the viewpoint of economic welfare. As we saw, Arrow gave five fair conditions which the voting system must meet. However, at the same time he showed that if these conditions are adhered to, there is no certainty that group decisions will be consistent in their outcomes. If collective transitivity is to be ensured, one of Arrow's conditions should be weakened.

The desire to ensure collective transitivity is, however, not the only argument to weaken one condition. The *fairness* of the 'fair' conditions is also disputed. The fairness of the third condition is especially questionable. This condition was that the outcome of a vote between two alternatives may depend only on the preferences which individuals have concerning *these two* alternatives. This means that the choice of the winning alternative is independent of irrelevant alternatives, i.e. of alternatives which have no chance. The condition is met when the choice from n alternative possibilities is made by choosing that particular alternative which gets the majority against $n-1$ alternatives. An imaginary series of contests (voting pair-wise) is organised and the only winner is the alternative which gains more than 50 per cent of the votes in every contest.

Arrow's preference for such contests is based on his assumption that the preferences of individuals are only ordered ordinally. This can be illustrated using the example given above (p. 34) of a canteen which serves only one type of roll. The canteen is visited now by three, not two, visitors of which one person (A) prefers ham rolls to cheese rolls, but both the others (B and C) prefer cheese rolls. The problem of whether cheese or ham rolls should be provided can now be solved by means of a vote. A contest between ham and cheese results in a majority for cheese. This is because every vote has an equal value and all that is important is the number of votes for ham or cheese. When this method is used, *the minority is always the loser*. This is valid as long as the preferences of A, B and C merely mean that two of them prefer cheese to ham, and that one prefers ham to cheese, i.e. as long as their preferences are merely ordered ordinally. However, as soon as A, B and C know the relative size of the differences in utility between ham and cheese, i.e. as soon as their preferences are ordered cardinally, it can be worth while to take the relative intensity of their preferences into account. In case of a cardinal preference ordering, the conclusion of Robert Dahl is applicable. When he examines in his book *A Preface to Democratic Theory* the problem of the intensity of policy preferences, he says succinctly that the researcher who ignores this intensity wrongly equates 'most preferred' and 'preferred by the most' (1956, p. 90).

The problem of the intensity of preferences is especially important in those cases where a relatively apathetic majority is faced by a very passionate minority. Dahl typified such a situation as a 'severe asymmetrical disagreement'. It is 'severe' because one of the groups is very passionate, 'asymmetrical' because the passions of one group contrast with the unconcern of the other. Figure 4.4 gives a graphic representation of a severe, asymmetrical disagreement. The graph shows that the proposal under discussion will be accepted by 55 per cent against 45 per cent. However, whereas 40 per cent are only slightly in favour of the proposal, 30 per cent are strongly opposed. If the voting had been limited to those passionately involved the proposal would have been defeated by a majority of 6:1.

Figure 4.4 *A severe, asymmetrical disagreement*

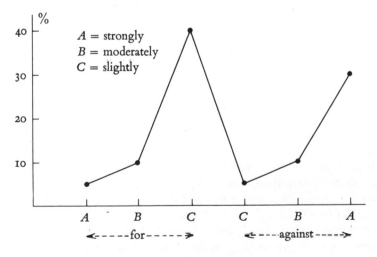

Source: Dahl, 1956, p. 99

When the intensity of policy preferences is ignored a host of welfare economic problems arise which I shall discuss in the remainder of this chapter. Seen from the point of view of economic welfare, the inclusion of the intensity of policy preferences in the process of decision-making is an improvement in terms of the neo-Paretian criterion. When the balance is not tipped towards a tepid majority but to a highly involved minority, the minority, if it is not too small, will easily be able to compensate the majority. Even after making such a compensation, the minority will still have a positive balance. The mere fact that the majority is tepid means that any relatively small compensation will be sufficient. When, on the other hand, a tepid majority forces its opinion on an impassioned minority, the majority will *not* succeed in compensating the minority. The fact that the minority is impassioned means that a very large compensation is necessary, so that the profit of the majority would be insufficient to finance these compensations.

Both tests of compensation point to the same conclusion: on the basis of the neo-Paretian criterion it would be an improvement if the intensity of the policy preferences were taken into account in the decision-making process.

Logrolling: an example

The voting system must thus solve two problems: to ensure collective transitivity and to take the relative differences in individual intensity into account. Both problems can be solved by changing the voting system. This will be discussed in the next subsection. However, the second problem can be solved within the framework of the existing voting system, by changing *political behaviour*. It is then a matter of finding a rule of behaviour in which the compensation of tepid majorities by impassioned minorities occurs automatically. This behaviour is called *logrolling* (vote trading) in the relevant literature. Logrolling means that the individuals concerned exchange their less urgent for their more urgent desires which means that, under certain conditions, an improvement will be brought about for the exchanging partners. For an exchange will take place only if the loss of utility experienced by the participating individuals is adequately compensated for. If all individuals participate in the exchange, the result could even be at an optimum for the whole group.

The effect on economic welfare of logrolling will be illustrated by an empirical example, that of an *historic compromise* reached between the Socialists and the Christian Democrats in the Netherlands in the beginning of the twentieth century. In Table 4.2 it has been assumed that at that time there were three groups of voters: Socialists, Liberals and Christian Democrats, each of which represented about one third of the Dutch voters. (The 'Liberal Democrats' who merged with the Socialists in 1946 have been included with the Socialists here.) At the beginning of the twentieth century there were two important questions in Dutch politics: the introduction of universal suffrage and the 'schools struggle' which was concerned with whether special (mainly Christian) schools would be given the same financial support as state-run schools. In Table 4.2 $a > b$ shows that a is preferred to b, while $a < b$ means that b is preferred to a. The sign $>$ means that the preference is tepid, while $>>$ indicates that the preference is strongly felt.

T ABLE 4.2 *Dutch policy preferences in 1913*

Groups	Relative size	Suffrage			Financing of special schools		
		universal (a)		limited (b)	equal (c)		discriminating (d)
Liberals	1/3	a	$<$	b	c	$<$	d
Socialists	1/3	a	$>>$	b	c	$<$	d
Christian Democrats	1/3	a	$<$	b	c	$>>$	d

Initially the Liberals were strongly opposed to the financial equation of state-run and special schools, but over the years their opposition gradually weakened. This is also true in respect of suffrage. In 1907 the De Meester Liberal Cabinet proposed some limited reforms to the voting system; these reforms were accepted by the Liberals, but as yet there was no movement in favour of universal suffrage.

The Socialists conducted a violent extra-parliamentary campaign for the introduction of universal suffrage. On the other hand, although they advocated putting the state-run schools in a privileged position, they were not strongly against equal rights for special schools.

The Christian Democrats fought passionately for the financial equation of state-run and special schools. Their position on suffrage was not clear. Initially the Protestants among them were in favour of a limited 'householders' suffrage' and the Roman Catholics were divided. The Christian Democrats, however, never campaigned against universal suffrage on principle.

At the beginning of the twentieth century the alternatives chosen were: 'limited suffrage' and 'financial discrimination against special schools'. This was also the case in the elections of 1913. Table 4.2 shows that limited suffrage won with the support of the Liberals and the Christian Democrats, while the financial discrimination of special schools won with the support of the Liberals and the Socialists. In the matter of suffrage the Socialists were a passionate minority, and in that of the special schools the Christian Democrats were a passionate minority. The Socialists and the Christian Democrats then logrolled in such a way that the Socialists agreed to support the financial equation of state-run and special schools, expecting the Christian Democrats to advocate the introduction of universal suffrage. This logrolling was not done explicitly but implicitly, e.g. by way of party congresses. As early as 1902 the SDAP Congress in Groningen passed an opportunist motion for the financial equation of state-run and special schools. In 1915 the extra-parliamentary Van der Linden cabinet set up a 'Conciliation Commission' to advise on the suffrage and the schools struggle. In the same year the Commission proposed to introduce a system of universal suffrage for men, based on proportional representation and compulsory voting. These proposals met with objections from the Christian Democrats. This criticism died down when, in 1916, the Commission recommended that state-run and special primary schools be given equal financial support. The Van der Linden Cabinet combined both proposals in 1917 in a proposal to revise the constitution so that both universal suffrage and the financial equation of state-run and special schools would become possible. The implicit logrolling now became apparent: the Socialists supported the financial equation of special schools and the Christian Democrats voted for universal suffrage to ensure that the revision of the constitution was accepted.

The logrolling meant that the utility of the Liberals declined. Thus the exchange was no improvement in terms of the criterion of Pareto. Whether it was an improvement in terms of the neo-Paretian criterion depended on whether the Socialists and Christian Democrat majority could compensate the Liberals. This would very probably have been the case. The Liberals had not had a strong preference for a specific policy on either the school struggle or universal suffrage, so the Socialists and the Christian Democrats would have needed to provide only a limited compensation to satisfy the Liberals.

This example has been simplified somewhat but it illustrates clearly that in general logrolling results in a majority vote for strongly preferred policy alternatives, precisely because the much desired points in the programme will form the contents of a negotiating offer and thus of a possible agreement. In the example, there were two groups of passionate minorities, the Socialists and the Christian Democrats, before logrolling; afterwards no group formed a passionate minority. As it may be assumed that the utility of those individuals who are freed from a passionate minority position will increase to such an extent that they will be able to give adequate compensation, logrolling will often satisfy the neo-Paretian criterion for optimum economic welfare – at least if a number of conditions are met, the most important of which is that the exchange situation must be a nonzero sum-game (see further: Mueller, 1976, pp. 406–7).

Alternative voting systems

In principle, logrolling makes it possible to solve the problem of taking individual intensity into account. Logrolling alone, however, does not ensure collective transitivity. If both problems are to be solved simultaneously, the voting system must be changed. Arrow's third condition of 'fairness', to the effect that the selection of a single policy alternative from n possibilities occurs in such a way that only that alternative is chosen which is the winner in a series of contests against each of the other $n-1$ alternatives, must then be discarded. The French mathematician De Borda (1781) designed an appropriate voting system which was later elaborated by Black (1971, pp. 59–66). Assume that five alternatives are being discussed, then the Borda method has two variants. The first means that voters place the alternatives in order of preference and give the most desired alternative 5 points, the second-highest 4 points, and so on. The alternative with the highest total is then the winner. In this example, each voter can allocate $5 + 4 + 3 + 2 + 1 = 15$ points. The second variant of the Borda method is that each voter can allocate his 15 points as he wishes, e.g. he can give all 15 points to one single alternative. The first variant is based implicitly on the assumption that an individual orders the alternatives according to an interval scale in which the difference in utility of two consecutive alternatives is always equidistant. When the second alternative is used, it is assumed that an individual is ordering his preferences on the basis of a ratio scale; if an alternative receives no points, it must then be concluded that the individual gains no utility from it.

Assume that the Liberals, the Socialists and the Christian Democrats could decide both questions at issue in the example in the previous paragraph using the second Borda criterion, whereby each individual can divide 5 points per question among the two alternatives. Assume further that the passionate always divide their points in the proportion 5:0 and the lukewarm in the proportion 3:2. In Table 4.3 universal suffrage would win with a majority of 9:6 from limited suffrage, whereas the financial equation of state-run and special schools would also win with a majority of 9:6 against the financial discrimination of special schools. In both cases the Borda method then achieves the same result as was achieved in the previous paragraph by logrolling. For the use of the points means that each policy alternative is given a certain weight and the complete ordering by individuals of preferences is totalled (Niemi and Riker, 1976, p. 25).

TABLE 4.3 *A historic compromise using the Borda method*

Groups	Relative size	Suffrage		Financing of special schools	
		universal	limited	equal	discriminating
Liberals	1/3	2	3	2	3
Socialists	1/3	5	0	2	3
Christian Democrats	1/3	2	3	5	0
Total*		9	6	9	6

* As all groups are equal in size, the number of points need not be weighted by the number of individuals belonging to a certain group.

Each voting method is based on a certain interpersonal evaluation of utility. Both the contests (pairwise voting) which Arrow advocates and the Borda method are based on the value judgment that the utility of each individual is of equal importance. After all, Arrow and De Borda award each individual the same number of votes. Whereas Arrow prefers a system of *one man, one vote*, De Borda's preference is for a system of, for example, *one man, ten votes*.

The literature contains innumerable objections to the Borda method (see, for example, Riker and Ordeshook, 1973, pp. 109–14; Niemi and Riker, 1976). The most important are that the method is vulnerable to strategic behaviour and manipulation. I shall illustrate both, using the example already given in Table 4.3 in which the second variant of the Borda method was applied. The objections, however, are also valid for the first variant.

Strategic behaviour means that voters do not vote in accordance with their real preferences. When, for example, the Liberals in Table 4.3 (page 91) are aware beforehand of the allocation of points by the Socialists and the Christian Democrats they can avoid a defeat by changing their allocation of points from 3:2 to 5:0. In this case the winners would have been neither universal suffrage nor the financial equation of state-run and special schools, but the continuation of limited suffrage and of the discrimination of special schools.

Manipulation of the voting results is possible in the Borda method by introducing a policy alternative which is irrelevant, i.e. which in itself has no chance. Because the Borda method abandons Arrow's third criterion which says that the result of a vote between two alternatives may depend only on the orderings of the individuals concerning *both these* alternatives, it is possible that the introduction of a third alternative will influence the decision fundamentally. Assume, for example, that the Liberals in the matter of suffrage introduce a new possibility, viz. universal suffrage based on a system of constituencies instead of proportional representation. Table 4.4 shows the possible outcome. As none of the three groups give the highest priority to the new alternative, it has no chance. Yet, the

TABLE 4.4 *The introduction of an irrelevant alternative*

Groups	Relative size	Universal suffrage (proportional representation)	Universal suffrage (constituencies)	Limited suffrage
Liberals	1/3	2	0	3
Socialists	1/3	3	2	0
Christian Democrats	1/3	0	2	3
Total		5	4	6

winner now is not universal suffrage but a limited suffrage. This is because the introduction of the new possibility has split the camp in favour of universal suffrage into two groups. Those opposing universal suffrage profit from this split.

This objection must be weighed against the objections inherent in other systems. Although Niemi and Riker reject the Borda method because of the way it can be manipulated, they note that 'no reasonable system of voting is immune to manipulation'. They conclude: 'One might want to rule out the most easily manipulated system, but among the less manipulable systems one should probably find some other standard for judging among them' (Niemi and Riker, 1976, pp. 25–6). In this chapter 'two other standards' have been discussed: preventing 'cycling' in majority decisions, and taking the urgent wishes of passionate minorities into account. Both criteria point towards a method comparable to the Borda system.

Everyone must be convinced of the need to ensure collective transitivity, but the desire to accommodate passionate minorities is still being questioned today. The author of this book would like to remind those sceptics of the words of President Madison of the United States who warned against a *tyranny of the majority*, and also of the conclusions drawn by Madison's kindred spirit, Hamilton (Dahl, 1956, p. 7): 'Give all power to the many, they will oppress the few.'

5

Representation

5.1 The demand for government policy

Elected representatives

In Chapter 4, I explained why, under certain conditions, an iron law of oligarchy operates in a direct democracy; this is because, in order to avoid high decision-making costs, all individuals accept a decision rule by which decisions are taken by a small group. This small group can consist of a minority which takes decisions completely independently of the other individuals. In a modern democracy, however, this small group consists of specialised 'agents' who have been chosen by all individuals. In such a case there is no longer any question of a direct democracy, but of an indirect or *representative* democracy. Largely following Buchanan and Tullock (1965, pp. 211–17), I understand representative democracy to be a method which on the one hand avoids the high costs of decision-making associated with a large number of decision-makers and, on the other hand, precludes the external costs associated with dictatorship or oligarchy.

In this chapter I shall assume that the individual voters will be represented by 'politicians' who combine the wishes of the voters and turn them into concrete proposals, weigh the interests of the various voters using 'interpersonal evaluations of utility', and decide on the proposals by a majority of votes. In this definition, the category of politicians includes: committee members of societies and political parties; members of community councils, of town councils, of county councils; parliament; the prime minister and, except in a presidential system, also the members of the cabinet.

In the literature the view predominates that representative democracy should be seen as an independent decision-making model. In this book, however, representation is taken to be an important part of the whole political process. This element is important because representation results in a clear *division between demanders and sup-*

pliers. In a negotiations democracy and in a referendum democracy each person is both a demander and a supplier. In a representative democracy individuals are specialised either as demanders or as suppliers.

In a representative democracy the demanders are private citizens. They want a variety of government services (social goods, income transfers) and are prepared to pay a certain price for them. In the traditional literature on public finance, it is assumed that this price consists exclusively of the payment of collective costs (taxes, social insurance premiums). There are, however, a number of government services which are not financed from taxes or premiums (e.g. an expansive government policy in a period of economic depression), and there are many voters who contribute little or nothing to collective costs, yet continue to be demanders. However, the price which the demanders pay in all cases is to give *political support* to certain politicians. For example, this support consists of voting for a certain political party. This section discusses the way in which the demanders exercise a demand in a representative democracy by providing political support.

Against the demanders, there are the suppliers who, in a representative democracy, are office-bearers, e.g. they have the office of elected representative or of civil servant. The role of civil servants will be discussed in Chapter 6, while this chapter deals with the elected representatives ('politicians'). The politicians supply the voters with a certain government policy in exchange for their support (i.e. their vote). The way in which this is achieved and what government policy results in an equilibrium between supply and demand is discussed in Section 5.2.

Finally, the degree to which the equilibrium resulting from the decision-making model of the representative democracy provides an optimum economic welfare, will be discussed in Section 5.3.

The influence of income

The exercise of a demand (the expression of wishes and the provision of support) is a form of political participation. In Chapter 3 attention was paid to the motives for *non-committed* participation where I concluded that in many cases, depending on policy preferences and the policy pursued, positive or negative apathy will dominate.

This conclusion is not shared by every investigator. In the political sciences it is customary to formulate the hypothesis that participation in politics depends largely on education and wealth so that the degree to which the various sectors of the population take part in politics differs and the highly paid in society will possess a relatively high degree of political influence. The question is thus to what extent the unequal distribution of certain resources (e.g. wealth) influences the outcome of the process of determining policy. It is not easy to answer this question. Even though studies in this field are being undertaken (see, for example, Salamon and Siegfried, 1977) we are still groping in the dark when it comes to the *absolute* influence of certain resources. However Breton (1974, pp. 74–105) has thrown some light on the *relative* influence of these resources by regarding political participation in a representative democracy as a set of various forms of action, both those which require commitment *and those which do not require commitment*. He distinguishes seven forms of political activity:

(1) participating in a pressure group or lobby;
(2) engaging in actions to influence politicians by direct contacts or by financial support;
(3) joining a social movement;
(4) evading and passing on government measures;
(5) providing a social good by a number of private persons;
(6) moving from one jurisdiction to another (voting with one's feet);
(7) giving one's support to a certain political party or not.

Breton puts the question as to what is the optimum combination of political instruments. All forms of participation cost time and money, though in differing combinations. He considers it possible to list various different combinations of political actions which are equally effective, beginning with the activity costing the most money yet requiring the least time and ending with the activity which costs the least money but requires most time. The individual optimum then depends on the *relative* availability of these resources. Voters with a very high income have *relatively* little time but a lot of money; the situation is often reversed for voters with a low income. If the effectiveness of the various combinations of activities is equal, voters with a high income will apply the relatively money-intensive methods, while voters with a low income will resort to relatively labour-intensive methods. This explains why the lower paid seldom attempt to bribe politicians or to migrate, and why the highest paid seldom attend political meetings, join in demonstrations, or sit-ins.

The concepts of 'left' and 'right'

In the rest of this chapter I shall confine myself to a single form of political participation, viz. the exercise of an effective demand by voting or abstaining from voting. The decision on whether or not to vote depends in the model given here solely on the basis of the voters' policy preferences and of the policy proposals of the various politicians. The idea that voters evaluate the various policy alternatives and vote in accordance with their findings is disputed (see Stigler, 1973). Barry (1970, pp. 165–83) reminds us that political thinkers such as De Maistre, Hegel and Coleridge considered the citizen to be fairly irrational in his behaviour. They did not expect that the citizen would make a sensible choice from the various strategies even when he had complete information at his disposal. These ideas led to remarks such as 'Roman Catholics always vote for Roman Catholics, no matter what policy is pursued'. This political tradition has been disputed by the publications of Campbell and others (1960) who argued that voters preferred candidates with whom they could identify even though not on the basis of all the policy proposals of the candidates, but on the basis of points of issue which happened to dominate the political scene at that moment. In the mid-1960s, however, the political sociologist Key concluded from empirical studies that what was until then considered an irrational identification with parties was in fact based on a weighing of policy alternatives in respect of the provision of social goods and the distribution of its costs: *'vote switches occur in directions consistent with the assumption that voters are moved by a rational calculation of the instrumental impact of their vote'* (Key, 1966, p. 47).

These policy preferences are often described by the terms 'left' and 'right'. Such terms are vague in three respects. First, no one is ever absolutely left or right but at most left or right *in relation to the average*. Second, in these terms no indication is given of the *degree* to which someone is left or right. Third, it must not be forgotten that the degree to which a person is left or right can vary *for each policy issue*.

In order not to complicate my analysis unnecessarily, I shall begin, following Downs (1957, pp. 116–17), with the assumption that elections are dominated by a single salient issue, e.g. by a complex of matters related to the question concerning the extent to which the government may limit the freedom of individuals. The first two objections to the vagueness of the terms 'left' and 'right' can be met by showing all possible policy preferences graphically in a *one-dimensional* continuum running from left to right as is shown in Figure 5.1. The preferences of persons A, B and C, who were chosen arbitrarily, are such that they are willing to reduce the absolute freedom of the individual by 20 per cent, 40 per cent, and 80 per cent respectively. From the figure it cannot be concluded whether B is left or right, but it is possible to determine that B is more left than C and more right than A, and also that C is more right than B, than A is more left than B.

Figure 5.1 *The political space*

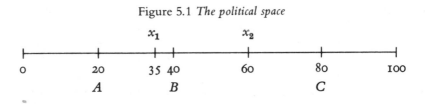

When there is more than one salient issue during the elections, then the political space can no longer be represented in one dimension by a single line. The political space must now be represented by a set of straight lines, in which each separate line represents a continuum from left to right of possible opinions on a single salient issue. Although the content of the analysis becomes more complicated, the method remains the same.

Neither, of course, does the method change when, as in Figure 5.1, not the policy ideas of just three voters are shown, but when the preferences of all voters are considered. As each voter can have a different idea about what would be the optimum policy, the policy optima of the voters can cover the whole continuum. The exact distribution of the voters over this continuum can be shown graphically by drawing a function $f(x)$ for each issue, which represents the relative number of voters who consider x the optimum policy.

Various assumptions are possible about the form of this function. This chapter is based largely on the work of pupils of Downs (1957), especially that of Riker, Hinich and Ordeshook (Riker and Ordeshook, 1968 and 1973; Davis, Hinich and Ordeshook, 1970; Hinich and Ordeshook, 1970; Ordeshook, 1976). They all invariably assume the shape of the function to be *symmetrical*. This means that every voter who prefers a certain policy has a counterpart in another voter who prefers a policy which is the diametric opposite.

A symmetrical distribution can be either unimodal or multimodal.

In this chapter I shall assume, in the first instance, that the voters' policy optima are distributed *unimodally* over the political space as is shown in Figure 5.2. A unimodal distribution assumes a certain consensus among the voters. This need not mean that most voters will prefer the policy of those political parties which present themselves as 'centre parties' but which aim primarily to uphold the existing social structure. It is also very probable that the consensus will be concentrated in a policy which will bend the existing structure in a progressive or reactionary direction. A unimodal distribution implies merely that there is only one *mode*.

Figure 5.2 *Distribution of policy optima*

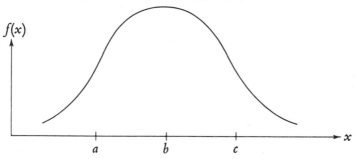

Indifference and alienation

Within the framework of the political space voters decide on how they will vote. In the model of Downs' followers (Riker and Ordeshook, 1973, pp. 62–9 and 322–39; Davis, Hinich and Ordeshook, 1970, p. 429; Hinich and Ordeshook, 1970, p. 775) voters first compare their own policy preferences with those of the various candidates, then they decide whether to vote or not, and then, finally, if they do vote, they will vote for the candidate whose policy is nearest to their own preference.

The decision to vote or to abstain from voting is based in the model on an individual cost–benefit analysis, in which the citizens weigh the following factors against one other:

P = the probability that the citizen will, by voting, materially affect the outcome of the election;

B = the differential benefit that he receives from the success of his preferred candidate over his less preferred one;

D = his personal satisfaction at having participated in the election;

C = the cost of voting;

and in such a way that the citizen only votes if:

$$PB + D - C > 0.$$

On the basis of this inequality, Riker, Hinich and Ordeshook conclude that there are two reasons why a voter could abstain, indifference and alienation.

Indifference occurs when all candidates propagate the same policy. From the viewpoint of individual voters, it then becomes immaterial which candidate is chosen, so that the value of B approaches zero. However, there is still a chance that the indifferent voter will vote: he will vote if $D - C > 0$, and in the opinion of the above-mentioned political scientists, D is relatively large. In Section 5.3 it will be shown that, in their view, indifference is related to positive apathy (see p. 51): 'You don't participate – this time – because you feel you can rely on the fact that those who do participate will arrive at a reasonably acceptable decision and because you are able to use the time to do something else which is more enjoyable.'

Alienation exists when the distance between one's own preference and that of any candidate whomsoever exceeds a certain critical limit. Because the voter does not recognise any of his own preferences in the proposed policies, he becomes demoralised, especially if his preferences are intense, and he loses faith in the democratic process. Even if the programmes of the various candidates differ, the voter still feels disheartened and useless, so that his feelings of personal satisfaction (D) approach zero. There is little likelihood that the alienated voter will vote: he will only vote if $PB - C > 0$, and Olson has already shown that P will always be low in a large group. In his opinion, political alienation corresponds with negative apathy, which was discussed in Chapter 3: 'When others have no sound policy, it is a waste of your time to try to change things.'

Empirical data

Hardly any serious attempts have been made to test separately all the hypotheses used in the theories discussed above to explain voters' behaviour. I have already mentioned an exception, Key's study of the voter's *policy orientation*. Irwin and Thomassen (1975) also studied the *distribution* of Dutch voters in respect of possible policy positions. Their questioning assumed the existence of a continuum of policy positions. They explained this continuum to those questioned by using a self-rating scale in which they were asked to indicate their own position as one of seven possible positions between clearly defined 'left' and 'right' positions (e.g. between: 'income differences should become smaller' and 'income differences should remain as they are'). It became apparent that the distribution of the voters along the continuum for one half of the issues involved was asymmetrical yet unimodal, and that the distribution of the other half was symmetrical yet bimodal or trimodal. However, this ambivalent result was partly due to the fact that the continuum was too much restricted by the questioning. When, for example, the left position is defined as 'income differences should become smaller' it is no surprise that most voters are on the extreme left. If, however, the left position had been defined as: 'income differences must be levelled down completely', then the advocates of a more equal income distribution would be spread (probably bell–shaped) over the different variants of a redistribution policy. The importance of a correct delineation of the left and right position is shown by Stapel, who (in 1974) also asked a number of Dutch voters to state whether they were left or right, but he in no way specified 'left' and 'right'. The distribution of the voters conformed almost entirely to the demands of unimodality and symmetry. All in all, it cannot be said that empirical studies of the separate hypotheses on which the Downsian model is based have led to a clear conclusion.

Shaffer (1972) tried to investigate the Downsian model as a whole, rather than as separate hypotheses, and to compare it with a much used sociological model. His conclusion was that, in respect of the American presidential elections in 1964, the *prediction* value of both models was about equal, but that the *explanatory* value of the economic model was by far the greater. In order to reach this conclusion he quantifies, in a primitive manner, the variables P, B, D and C used in the economic model. According to Shaffer, the voter's estimation of the probable influence his vote would have on the election outcome (P) was dependent on the degree to which the outcome of the election would be close and was therefore measured by him as the margin by which, in the eyes of the voter, one of the rivals would win. Shaffer based the estimated increase in his utility, should the preferred candidate win (B), on the degree of concern of the voter over the election outcome and the effect of this outcome on his personal wealth. Shaffer measured the personal satisfaction of the voter (D) using questions as to whether voters believed that elections were important in maintaining democracy, while he obtained the cost of voting (C) by calculating the time spent in collecting information on the salient issues from the media.

Shaffer then applied a computer simulation. As was to be

expected, this showed that variable *C* (specified in terms of the use of
the media) disturbed the reliability of the model so that this variable
was deleted from the model after some discussion. It *then* became
clear that the economic and the sociological models could predict
correctly no less than 66.6 per cent and 69.5 per cent respectively of
the outcome of the election. Both models were unreliable on the
same point: both badly underestimated the number of abstentions.
The simulation also provided separate conclusions on the relative
importance of each variable individually. In the economic model the
variable *P* (the extent to which the election will be close) could be
disregarded without affecting the reliability. On the other hand, a
correct estimate of the voters' personal satisfaction (*D*) and the
elimination of *C* (discussed above) were of the utmost importance
for the predictability of the economic model. However, the reliability of the prediction was not affected in the sociological model by
the deletion of any variable whatsoever. Shaffer holds that this could
be explained by the fact that ultimately all variables represent the
same phenomenon, the loyalty of a voter to a certain party. This
overlap of factors means that the sociological model, despite its
acceptable level of predictability (which is based on correlations), can
only provide a poor explanation of cause and effect in voting
behaviour.

TABLE 5.1 *Simulation of the American presidential elections
in 1964*

choices	voters in %		
	prediction		outcome
	economic model	sociological model	
Democratic party	67.7	63.5	53.4
Republican party	29.5	28.6	25.7
abstentions	2.8	7.9	20.9
correctly predicted	66.6	69.5	

Source: Shaffer, 1972, pp. 107 and 121

5.2 The supply of government policy

The aims of politicians

Confronting voters' demand for a certain government policy there is a corresponding supply by politicians. During an election the supply can be seen in the form of policy proposals which are presented to the voters alongside those of competing candidates. Of course, the decisions on these proposals are directed at achieving certain aims. In the previous section I assumed that the *voters*, by voting, attempted to direct government policy in the direction of a policy optimum. Following Downs, Riker, Hinich and Ordeshook, I, too, will assume that the *candidates* using their policy proposals will try to direct the voters in the direction of an electoral optimum. In the opinion of the voter, a policy is at an optimum when economic welfare, as he sees it, is maximised. In the opinion of the candidate an election result is at an optimum when he receives sufficient support to be able to participate as effectively as possible in government.

The idea that a politician aims at an electoral optimum needs further elucidation. In my opinion, politicians can be divided into careerists and paternalists (see also Hoogerwerf, 1971, p. 110). The pure careerist maximises the number of votes given to himself, to his party or to his regular coalition partners. The pure paternalist has 'merit wants': he maximises the level of a set of values which are determined not so much by the voters as autonomously. The concept of a careerist is most closely related to American politics; the concept of a paternalist to European politics, even though just before the actual elections a large number of careerists suddenly appear in European countries as well.

There is not necessarily always a clear distinction between the two ideal types. The careerist regards electoral support as an aim and the policy as a means. The paternalist, on the other hand, sees the policy as an aim and electoral support as a means. Under certain conditions the result is the same. As long as a politician does not have a monopoly position, obtaining electoral support is vital for him in order to realise the policy he prefers. Should a paternalist ignore this fact, he will be defeated by his opponent, and he will then be rudely awakened. When the candidates are able to obtain governing power solely *by means of a competitive struggle for the people's vote*, the paternalist will feel obliged, on pain of the liquidation of his political power, to act as a careerist. The policy that he desires remains his basic motivation, but the support he must gain is his immediate motivation on the basis of which his behaviour can be described and predicted.

Riker and Ordeshook (1973, pp. 335–6) have suggested that the exact nature of the careerist's aims will depend on the party system. In a *multi*party system parties or candidates can only take part in the government by forming a coalition and the more votes they collect so their position in a coalition becomes stronger. It can therefore reasonably be assumed that, in the period preceding an election, candidates in a multiparty system maximise the number of votes given to them and the number of votes cast in favour of their opponents does not matter. However, in a *two*party system the situation is completely different. Here the candidate is not so much concerned with getting more votes, irrespective of the electoral position of his opponent, but with defeating his opponent. The logical result, according to Riker and Ordeshook, is that in a twoparty system, candidates do not strive to obtain an absolute maximum of votes, but to achieve the greatest possible *majority* (plurality).

The dynamics of political parties

The models used by Downs, Riker, Hinich and Ordeshook to ana-lyse the political strategies of candidates are derived from the geometric model Hotelling used in the 1930s to examine the location of grocers in a certain catchment area. In Hotelling's model the number of consumers supplied by a grocer varies with his geo-graphical location. In the models of Downs, etc. the number of voters represented by a candidate varies with the political location of this candidate, i.e. with his policy proposals in respect of a number of independent issues. From now on I shall call such a political location a *platform*. In order to simplify my analysis, I shall begin by assuming that the elections are dominated by a single issue.

As regards the candidates the authors mentioned above assume that their platform is completely mobile, with the single restriction that the candidates cannot pass each other. The optimum platform of a candidate *in a multiparty system* is then determined by the tension between convergent and polarising forces. Attention will first be paid to the converging forces. When a candidate (for example in a threeparty system) having a monopoly of the left-hand side of the continuum, evolves in the direction of the mode, he will lose the votes of the extreme left-wing voters who feel politically alienated. Initially he will win more right-wing voters than he loses in left-wing voters because there are, after all, more voters near the mode than there are far away from it. The same argument applies to a candidate who occupies a monopoly position on the right-hand side of the continuum. On balance, evolution towards the mode results in an advantage for extreme candidates with a monopoly position. On the basis of the model, partial convergence can always be predicted in a multiparty system.

But no complete convergence occurs because there are also forces at work which favour a permanent policy distance between the candidates. If two or more candidates approach the mode they must share the modal voters. They no longer win and lose votes only in a no-man's-land, they also do so at the expense of one another's monopolised votes. Thus they are no longer in a monopoly position, but they compete. Furthermore, the closer a candidate comes to the mode, the greater is the number of extreme voters he must forgo. Thus, when the evolution towards the mode has reached a certain point, the gain in votes from modal voters no longer compensates for the loss of votes from extreme voters. Once this point is reached, it is no longer worth while to evolve further: the extreme candidate in a monopoly position is now in equilibrium.

This situation changes as soon as the monopoly of the former extremist is broken by the entry of a new extremist candidate. The former extremist can now do one of two things: either he can try to restore his monopoly or he accepts its loss. In the former case he returns temporarily to his extremist base in order to defeat the newcomer or to join forces with him, and thereafter he will return to his natural point of equilibrium. In the latter case he will evolve completely to the mode, because now that he has competition on both his left and right wing, his reason for preserving a policy distance to his opponents in the centre no longer applies, since there are more voters near the mode than far away from it. As soon as he reaches the mode he will either defeat his opponents there or he will join them. In the meantime the new extremist, who now occupies a monopoly among the extremist voters will move (for the reasons given at the beginning of this subsection) towards the equilibrium position of his predecessor, so that the whole story will repeat itself. I have now, somewhat crudely, expressed the unambiguous result of Hinich and Ordeshook's mathematical calculations (1970, p. 787): that in a multiparty system in equilibrium three different political locations remain. In Figure 5.2 (p. 99) these are, for example, the platforms *a*, *b* and *c*. It is not necessary that each platform be occupied by a single candidate or party. It is equally possible that on one of the platforms more candidates or parties are located who agree to cooperate on a regular basis.

Inconsistency and unreliability

In 1957 Downs stressed that in a threeparty system it was practically impossible for voters to order their preferences rationally. After all, a parliamentary majority is a minimum requirement to be able to form a stable government. He illustrates the problems arising from a threeparty system using Figure 5.1 (p. 98) in which A, B and C represent the three candidates who have occupied a certain political platform. Under these circumstances there are many ways of arriving at a majority. However, in a study of coalition theories, De Swaan (1973, p. 288) showed that not all possibilities will be used. A party will only join a coalition with parties which have the nearest platforms and, in addition, it will not join any coalition larger than is absolutely necessary to obtain a majority. In the example given in Figure 5.1 this means that coalition AC is ruled out so that, to begin with, five possibilities remain to achieve a majority: A, B, C, AB and BC. In the last two cases, concerning the coalition between a centre candidate and one of the relatively extreme candidates, one candidate can either dominate the other (e.g. Christian Democrat–Labour or Labour–Christian Democrat) or both candidates can have equal influence. Each coalition thus has three variants which means that there are nine possibilities: A, B, C, AB, aB, Ab, BC, bC and Bc.

Uncertainty arises because the coalition existing before the elections is not necessarily the same as that existing after the elections. Assume that voter x_1 in Figure 5.1 votes for candidate B because B approaches his own optimum most closely. However, when B forms a coalition BC after the elections, the policy pursued will approach x_2. If x_1 had known about the coalition beforehand, he would not have voted for B but for A, because A approaches his optimum more closely than does x_2.

The continuing need to form a coalition means that, in the words of Downs (1957, pp. 105–7), the candidates become inconsistent and unreliable. *Inconsistency* here means that at the beginning of a new parliamentary session the candidates do not accept responsibility for the policies pursued in the previous period. *Unreliability* here means that the outcome of an election gives no definite answer as to what policies will be pursued by the new parliament. As a result voters are often forced to take non-rational decisions.

In order to combat this evil, the 'neo-democrats' in the Netherlands (see page 52) have, since 1966, often pleaded for the introduction of new rules of procedure which will provide that the election programmes of the coalition partners cannot be the subject of political negotiations after the elections. As a result, during the elections for the Second Chamber in 1971 and 1972 an attempt was made to agree on the future cabinet before the election. In 1971 the socialists (PvdA), the radical liberals (D'66) and the ecologists (PPR) presented a complete shadow cabinet. Before the elections in 1972 it was considered sufficient to present only a few of the shadow cabinet, but the few were furnished with a complete policy agreement on which they could not – except for actual technical points – negotiate with the other parties. Prior to the elections in 1977 the PvdA and the PPR agreed that they would only participate in a new government if their ministers had a majority at cabinet meetings.

The traditional method of forming a cabinet is a result of the existing multiparty system, whereas the introduction of agreements before the elections should be seen as an attempt to break open the multiparty system and to arrive at two parties or two permanent coalitions which will destroy the 'political centre' and provide the voters with a clear choice between *two essentially different policy alternatives*. According to the political reformers the polarisation of power is thus a way to achieve a polarisation of policy.

Policy polarisation

The expectation of a twoparty system entertained by the Dutch political reformers is not realised in the models discussed. In a system with two candidates, a candidate does not strive simply to maximise his votes but to defeat his rival. His success thus depends not only on the additional votes he receives, but also on the number of votes his opponent loses. Riker and Ordeshook have argued persuasively that the stimulus to converge is much greater in a twoparty than in a threeparty system. When the two candidates move towards the mode, then, in the first place, the loss by the one candidate of his extremist supporters is completely compensated by a corresponding loss on the part of his opponent. In the second place, every vote which a candidate gains from his rival near the mode is doubly important to him: such a vote is not only added to his total but is also deducted from his rival's total (Riker and Ordeshook, 1973, p. 350, n. 14).

The outcome of the models considered above is that when one

candidate assumes a position at the mode and the other does not, then the modal candidate will in all cases receive the majority of votes. Thus, he who evolves most rapidly to the mode has the greatest certainty that he will defeat his rival. Under these circumstances both rivals will want to be on the safe side and will occupy platforms on the mode. As a result, their policy will be subject to a process of complete convergence so that there is no question of a supply of 'two fundamentally different policy alternatives'. It is not the platforms at the centre which are destroyed in this model, but the platforms located to the left and right. Hotelling illustrates this by the example of two shopkeepers who, in a main street which is equally busy throughout its length, both decide to locate their shops in the middle of the street.

When the elections are dominated not by one issue but by a number of issues, the argument remains the same. In this case, the political space must not be seen as one straight line running from left to right, but by a set of left to right dimensions in which each dimension represents an independent salient political issue. When the relative importance of all issues is the same, viz. when voters give all issues *the same relative weight*, then the policy outcome of a twoparty system is the *modal opinion of each dimension*.

It is probably superfluous to use a complicated mathematical model to arrive at the same conclusion. After all, the possibility of complete convergence in a twoparty system is arguable on grounds of pure logic. According to Riker and Ordeshook (1973, pp. 343 and 348), however, the mathematical model also enables the less trivial conclusion to be drawn that, even when we drop the assumption of a unimodal distribution of voters' policy preferences, under certain conditions there will still be a complete convergence of both candidates. These conditions are:

(1) the distribution of policy preferences is bimodal and symmetric;
(2) the voters' utility functions have a 'concave' or a 'quasi-concave' shape which means that as the distance between the policy desired by the voter and the policy pursued by the politicians increases, the utility of the voter decreases more than proportionately.

That there may be no supply of 'two fundamentally different policy alternatives' even when the distribution of policy preferences is bimodal is a conclusion which makes Carlyle's remark about economics being a dismal science still very much to the point.

Some empirical evidence

Robertson (1976) attempted to test the Downsian predictions of the platforms occupied by the Labour and Conservative parties in Britain in the general elections of 1924 to 1966.

The most important raw material for his analysis consisted of the official party manifestos of both parties. The central party manifestos were chosen because they are the only direct and clear statements of party policy available to the electorate which are directly attributable to the party. Though it is perhaps unlikely that they are read by many voters, they are the official source of the impressions the electorate have of the parties' platforms.

As the period discussed is very long, Robertson searched for policy-dimensions which represented the basic structure of policy competition throughout the entire period. Therefore, 'issues' as such are not eligible, as they are too specific. Tariff-reform was a pre-war issue, comprehensive education a post-war one; at other times both were non-starters. Obviously Robertson could not replace 'issues' by full-blooded ideological statements. To have done so would have been to force documents which are essentially pragmatic into a too theoretical mould.

Instead Robertson examined the documents for references to 'topics' or 'symbols': these ranged from an insistence on aspects of socialist economic policy (e.g. nationalisation), or its opposite *laissez-faire* symbol of de-restriction, to foreign affairs with symbols such as 'faith in the empire', or 'collective security as the mainspring of peace and safety'. He then coded each manifesto, counting the number of times each symbol occurred. A final score sheet for a manifesto, expressed as a percentage of the total number of relevant symbols (to standardise for length and verbosity) thus provides a measure of the relative frequency of symbols. Robertson believed this to account for the basics of policy debate over a period of forty-two years which included some of the most violent social upheavals.

Factor analysis enabled Robertson to reduce the sets of symbols to seven dimensions of British politics. The first two were of the greatest importance. Together they account for nearly 50 per cent of the common variance. These two major dimensions of political conflict are economic in nature. The first concerns *long-term* economic policy. It reveals the conflict over the method society should adopt for handling its economic problems. Symbols such as 'economic orthodoxy', 'incentives' and 'enterprise' are juxtaposed with 'socialist economics', 'economic planning' and 'social justice'. The second dimension reflects the tensions in *short-run* economic policy. Here the stress placed on the adequacy of the economy ('you've never had it so good') is opposed to the stress put on the need for restrictions and sacrifices.

Robertson draws many interesting conclusions from his analysis, only two of which will be discussed here. They concern the mobility and convergence of both parties (see Figure 5.3).

The first conclusion is that the parties are *mobile*, i.e. they change their positions nearly every four years: now to the left, now to the right. Robertson argues that this inconsistent behaviour is in no way compatible with the 'alternative thesis' on party behaviour. This alternative thesis is a model of a 'sincere' party: one which resolutely sticks to a policy platform its members believe in, and which it will not alter until objective conditions change.

The second conclusion is that the positions of both parties tend *to come nearer to each other* in six of the seven dimensions. To quote Robertson (1976, p. 102): 'There is little doubt that a process of convergence has taken place over time.' No convergence occurred in respect of the seventh dimension because the positions here had already approximated each other before the Second World War. This process of convergence corroborates roughly the Downsian theory of party competition.

However, on several of the dimensions the convergence has been only partial. A complete convergence had not occurred at the end of the period analysed (1966). Robertson sought an explanation of this phenomenon in a number of factors, of which the most important was that until the 1960s the grass roots of the Conservative Party formed a loyal vote-block, within certain limits irrespective of the party's precise policies. As a result, between 1924 and 1966 the Conservatives could often afford to occupy a relatively extreme platform without endangering their election majority.

The assumptions of the model

Robertson's book is a reminder that the conclusions drawn so far in this chapter depend on the assumptions on which the Downsian model is based (for a complete list see Ordeshook, 1976). The most important assumptions are:

(1) The voters evaluate the politicians solely on the basis of their policy stands (p. 97).

Figure 5.3 *Changes in British party positions 1924–66*

(a) Changes in long-term economic policy

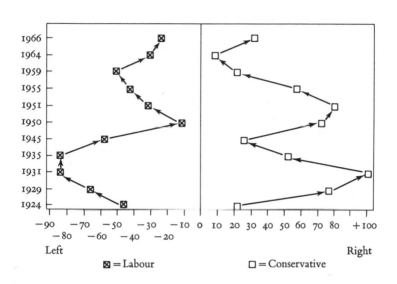

(b) Changes in short-term economic policy

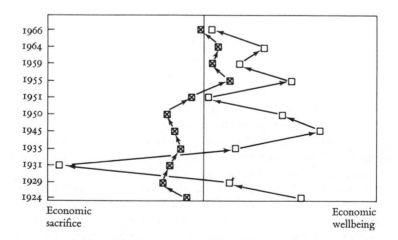

Source: Robertson, *A Theory of Party Competition* (1976), John Wiley and Sons, Ltd, Chichester (1976), pp. 98 and 101

(2) The set of political platforms can be represented by a space of straight lines running from left to right (p. 98).

(3) Every voter has a utility at each point on these lines (p. 20).

(4) These utility functions have a 'concave' or a 'quasi-concave' shape, which means, among other things, that there is only one policy which is an optimum for the voter.

(5) The optima of the individual voters are distributed symmetrically over the political space (p. 98).

(6) Voters can abstain from voting because they are indifferent or alienated (pp. 99–100).

(7) The politicians aim to win the elections to enable them to (continue to) participate in government (p. 103).

(8) The platforms taken by the politicians on each of the (policy) lines are completely mobile, with the restriction that politicians cannot pass each other (p. 104).

(9) The voters give the same relative weight to all issues (p. 108).

(10) There is perfect competition among the political parties (pp. 117–18).

(11) Politicians have complete information on the voters' utility functions and the voters have perfect information on the benefits and costs inherent in the platforms of the politicians (pp. 118–19).

The first seven assumptions have already been discussed in earlier paragraphs. The eighth assumption (on mobility) will be discussed below. The last three assumptions (9, 10 and 11) will be examined extensively in the third section of this chapter, which deals with democracy and economic welfare.

The assumption of perfect mobility has been criticised sharply by Hirschman (1970, pp. 70–2). In his opinion, Riker et al. were too greatly influenced by Hotelling, who described a market system in which the consumer was powerless as to where shopkeepers located their shops. After all, in the model consumers had nowhere else to go. But, according to Hirschman, voters are not powerless in a democracy. Did Robert Dahl not say that nearly everyone has access to many still unused political resources? This applies in particular to activists among the party officials, who have an important influence on the election of candidates and on the organisation of the election campaign. In Hirschman's view they will do everything to prevent their party from occupying a standpoint they detest. He therefore considers perfect mobility of political parties a naive assumption.

Representation 113

Hirschman also argues that assumption no. 9 must be rejected, i.e. that all voters give the same relative weight to all issues. In the following section the consequences of such a rejection will be analysed. However, insofar as Hirschman's argument is more than a simple rejection of assumption no. 9, it conflicts with the picture I gained from my own observations during my term as a member of the Dutch parliament. The argument most frequently used (even by parties dominated by a strong ideology) to convince a certain party cadre of the (in)correctness of a specific strategy, is a reference to the electoral effect of such a strategy. Party cadres generally rebel only when the election looks like being lost or has already been lost. Of course, a party can, under the influence of activist cadres, take a decision which is undesirable from an electoral point of view. Among the examples most frequently given of such a wrong decision, are two from the USA: Goldwater's republican candidacy for the presidency in 1964, and McGovern's democratic candidacy in 1972. However, such a mistake is immediately punished with an overwhelming defeat so that the other, more mobile party, takes over the government. In a party system based on a fair degree of competition, immobile parties either become mobile or disappear.

5.3 Democracy and economic welfare

Democracy and the Pareto criterion

In Chapter 2, I formulated the conditions under which economic welfare, insofar as it depends on the provision of public goods and services, is at an optimum on the basis of the (neo-)Paretian criterion. I shall now consider if the institutions of representative democracy, discussed above, give a guarantee that these conditions will be met.

In any case, a multiparty system does not give this guarantee. In such a system, three platforms will be maintained in equilibrium in which each platform is occupied by one party or by a group of parties which make a ballot-box agreement among themselves. Such ballot-box agreements are a useful means of preventing the number of independent parties from becoming larger than is necessary for a clear presentation of the three policy alternatives, so that they make a substantial contribution to the rationality of the democratic process. But the need to form a cabinet after the elections generally remains in a threeparty system. From the viewpoint of the rational voter, the parties, as they present themselves before the elections, thus become inconsistent and unreliable. The policy outcome of a threeparty system is indeterminate and the certainty that this result is at an optimum on the basis of the Paretian criterion cannot be guaranteed at all. Tinbergen's conclusion (1965, p. 738) that the number of parties should be equal to the number of independent issues in economic policy, does not sufficiently take into account the unpredictability of the coalition which must be formed and the subsequent indeterminedness of the policy outcome; I shall therefore discard it.

In a twoparty system the outcome of an issue is usually predetermined. Downs (1957, p. 181) has suggested that this outcome, provided that political competition is perfect and that political information is complete, will be Pareto optimal. Shubik (1968) has confirmed the accuracy of Downs' conclusion. After all, a Paretian improvement is an improvement in the position of some without a worsening in the position of others. Such an improvement always provides a gain in votes in the model discussed above. Should one of the two parties not choose a Pareto-optimal location, it could always be defeated by a rival who does.

When discussing the question whether a twoparty system is at an optimum from society's point of view, a distinction must be made between two cases. First, the voters consider all issues to have the same relative importance. This is, as already seen, assumption no. 9 of Riker, etc. In the second case a number of voters give some issues a greater relative importance than other voters do. This, for example, is the assumption I put forward in Section 4.3.

The first case is elaborated by Riker and Ordeshook (1973, pp. 373–5). When the political space must be presented as a set of left to right dimensions in which each dimension represents a separate issue, the policy outcome of a twoparty system lies on the median of each dimension. Riker and Ordeshook then ask the question: if a society were to be governed by an omniscient and benevolent dictator (e.g. Plato's philosopher–king of the *Republic* mentioned in Chapter 2) who would give an equal weight to the utility of each voter in determining his economic policy objective function, and who would then maximise this function, what policy would then be the best for the dictator? The answer is as follows. If we now assume that the citizens' utility functions are concave (assumption no. 4) and that the distribution of the citizens' policy preferences is symmetric (unimodal or bimodal), then the philosopher–king would select the median of each dimension as the optimum policy. An omniscient and benevolent philosopher–king then would not mind delegating the decisions on the social goods to a twoparty political system which is highly competitive.

Democracy and the neo-Paretian criterion

Riker and Ordeshook's assumption about the relative importance of all issues being equal, is unrealistic. The second case is of greater importance and it also fits in with the problems I discussed in Chapter 4. When some voters are passionate in respect of certain problems, the chance of a candidate winning an election increases considerably when he combines issues and thus implicitly applies logrolling. Such implicit logrolling can take place between different parties but also within one party, which, after all, can be seen as a permanent coalition of various social groups. Hirschman in fact also pointed to the existence of implicit logrolling (p. 112). It is always possible for a candidate to bind a minority, which is passionate in respect of a single issue, to him by meeting its wishes on this one point *provided that the majority, which he goes against is relatively uninterested*. Nevertheless to prevent him losing this majority to his opponent, he will have to accommodate this majority on other matters which it considers to be of especially great importance.

Van Thijn (1967, pp. 59–61) has shown that historically the twoparty system derived its specific nature from such logrolling. He harks back to the period 1721–42 when Robert Walpole held the reins of government and obtained an iron grip on the majority in parliament, partly through corruption. According to Van Thijn this had nothing to do with parliamentary democracy. Parliamentary democracy only came into being when the first leader of the opposition (Bolingbroke) succeeded in transforming the diversity of the groups of people, who were united solely by the fact that they had freed themselves from Walpole's powerful grip, into a more or less coherent opposition, which slowly developed into a majority which brought about Walpole's downfall in 1742.

Logrolling has a consequence which Downs and his followers missed: under conditions to be discussed later *a twoparty system tends to achieve unanimity by the use of implicit logrolling.* Had a twoparty system existed in the Netherlands at the beginning of the twentieth century, the elections would have been won by the politicians (or the statesman) who combined the introduction of universal suffrage and the financial equation of state and church schools in a single platform (see pp. 87–90). In Chapter 4, I showed that such logrolling could lead to an increase in economic welfare in terms of the neo–Paretian criterion. In the example, the liberals remained a minority but their loss in utility has been compensated by later statesmen, viz. by increasing the cultural freedom for which the liberals strove passionately and against which the Christian Democrats had no fundamental objections. In this case, economic welfare will be increased by each *new* case of logrolling until the optimum is reached. Of course, this conclusion applies, on the condition that during this process of logrolling, which will take many years, no new issues are created.

From the above examples it becomes apparent that the abandonment of assumption no. 9 ('the voters give the same relative weight to all issues') has important consequences for the policy outcome in a representative democracy. After logrolling has taken place, the policy outcome no longer always lies at the mode of every policy line but, depending on the issues involved, to the left or right of it. The 'political centre' (the 'modal' policy) is destroyed by compromising or by forming coalitions. However, this is not a result of little, but of great mobility.

Finally, I conclude that in a democratic process, a twoparty system stimulates most the attainment of an optimum economic welfare. Under the conditions nos. 10 and 11 a twoparty system produces the same optimum as would be reached by the decisions of an omniscient and benevolent philosopher–king who would give equal weight to the utility of each voter. When I assess a twoparty system using a (neo-)Paretian standard, the outcome of the decision-making process in a democracy is such that no voter can improve his position further without worsening that of another, and those voters who have improved their position at the expense of other voters would be able to compensate the losers completely. This conclusion applies not only to democracy in government, but also to democracy in clubs and in firms. In the case of a club, it would be worth while, in pursuit of an economic welfare optimum, if the candidates for office were to merge into two competing groups. In an election for a workers' council, which is made up corporatively of two groups (employers and employees), the attainment of an optimum welfare of the groups is stimulated when *each* group submits *two* lists of candidates, so that two candidates compete for the votes *of each group*.

Political competition

The most important assumption on which the model is based is that of perfect political competition (assumption no. 10). Frey (1970b) in particular made it clear that Riker et al. presented a model of *pure* democracy, which can be compared with the model of a market operating under perfect competition. At first this seems a strange conclusion. In a market, perfect competition is characterised by a large number of suppliers. In the political process pure democracy is characterised by the existence of only two political parties. The difference between these models is less important, however, than their similarity: *in an optimum situation no one has any power*. In the market model the absence of economic power results from *economic* indifference; the consumers are indifferent to where they buy their goods at the current market prices and the producers (since in the long run profits will be zero) are indifferent to whether they produce in the same industry or not. In the political model the absence of political power manifests itself in *political* indifference. The voters are indifferent because, no matter which candidate is chosen, their utility will not be affected. The paternalists are indifferent because the policy is the same no matter whether they or their rivals govern. Only the careerists are interested in the outcome of the elections.

Another common characteristic of the models for a competitive market and for a pure democracy is that the optimum situation is achieved only when a number of ideal conditions have been met. For the political model, I summarised the most important of these conditions in Section 5.2. Two of these conditions must be considered more closely: that of perfect political competition and that of perfect political information.

Perfect competition here does not mean an active rivalry. Actually, the political equilibrium in which two parties offer the same programme is very boring. A voter interested in politics will get the feeling that there is no competition at all and that the parties have formed a tacit coalition. All that is meant by 'perfect competition' is what Schumpeter (see p. 13) described as an institutional structure in which political power is in the hands of a large number of anonymous voters. This institutional structure is an ideal which is characterised by the *continued occurrence of elections*. Only when elections are held regularly do the political parties themselves have no power at all.

The competition between politicians is, of necessity, perfect during the election campaigns. After all, in a twoparty system the election is a *zero-sum game*: what the one wins, is lost by the other. But as soon as the elections have been held, the stake is no longer a gain in votes but paternalistic policy satisfaction. The game then becomes a *nonzero-sum game*: more satisfaction for the one does not necessarily mean less satisfaction for the other. In such a case a restriction of competition can be beneficial to both parties (Wittmann, 1973, p. 497). Just as oligopolies may reduce their price competition in the commodities market and maximise their sales, it is conceivable that in a twoparty system both parties will keep the costs of social goods out of the political arena and will stress the benefits of these goods. Lindblom (1968), among others, observed such conflict-minimising behaviour in respect of costs. In my opinion, this must be seen as a manifestation of political power resulting from the fact that all parties have little interest in gaining votes in the period between elections. The less attention politicians need to pay to the electoral effects of their policy, the greater the chance that social goods will be provided in non-optimum amounts at non-optimum prices.

Political information

The model of pure democracy is based not only on perfect competition but also on perfect information (assumption no. 11). Politicians are assumed to be informed about the voters' utility functions and voters about the benefits and costs of social goods. Berg (1975) clearly summarised the arguments why neither assumption is valid. Not only is it virtually impracticable to obtain information about the marginal benefits and disadvantages of a social good for each individual, but it is also theoretically not feasible. If a voter wants others to pay for a social good, he will hide his preference for that good. If he especially wants his individual wishes to be taken account of, he will exaggerate the urgency of his wishes.

The information voters have about the benefits and costs of social goods is also usually poor. According to Downs (1965) the benefits of some social goods are far removed in time or space from the voter: these are 'hidden benefits' for the voters. Examples of this include: town and country planning, energy policy, development aid, and foreign policy. To this I must add that there are also hidden costs: people are aware of indirect taxation, for example, only when the rates are raised or lowered. There is also the possibility that voters will see only the benefits of some goods and only the costs of other goods. In the former case they will support a utopian policy, i.e. a policy with detailed information about the aim, but with no information about the means of realising this aim. In the second case, they will vote for a technocratic policy in which the emphasis lies primarily on the means, but where the aims are kept vague.

In these cases there is no reason at all why the politician who wants to maximise the number of votes cast for him should strive for an optimum economic welfare. Paternalist politicians run the risk of being defeated by their opponents unless they also succeed in hiding their paternalism from the voters. In particular, it is impossible to conduct a long-term policy as long as the voters are geared to the short term. Statesmen who, in the words of a famous definition, do not plan for the next election but for the next generation, will, in the model, disappear very quickly indeed. The consequences of this can easily be imagined. De Tocqueville (1835; 1948, pp. 129 and 137) wrote about democracy in the United States: 'At the approach of an election the head of the executive government thinks only of the struggle ahead; he no longer has anything to look forward to; he can undertake nothing new.' And: 'It is impossible to consider the ordinary course of affairs in the United States without perceiving that the desire to be re-elected is the chief aim of the President; that the whole policy of his administration, and even his most indifferent measures, tend to this object; and that especially as the crisis [i.e. the election] approaches, his personal interest takes the place of his interest in the public good.' Unless the voters either take a long view or can always remember which party in the past pursued policies directed at the future, each actual system of representative democracy has the built-in tendency *for the government's policy horizon to be no longer than the period between two elections.*

This peculiarity is the reverse of the structure discussed in the previous paragraph in which elections are continually taking place. If the period between two elections is long, this will reduce political competition. But if this period is short, then government policy *in a real society* will be dominated by the short-sightedness of the voters. As long as the voters do not take a long view or have a good memory, this dilemma is insoluble and the actual period of parliament will always be characterised by compromise.

The weak future-directedness of an actual democracy has for centuries been an argument for rejecting democracy as a method of decision-making. Dahl (1970, p. 8) contributed to this discussion by formulating three criteria for deciding whether to accept a process for making decisions, the elements of 'personal choice', 'economy' and 'competence'. The criterion of *personal choice* contains the requirement that individuals as the consumers and producers of social goods are sovereign in making the decisions. The criterion of *economy* requires that the decision-making process respects the scarcity of time and energy of the citizen. The criterion of *competence* demands that those who take the decisions have sufficiently expert knowledge and moral fitness.

Although Dahl's criteria were designed for another purpose, I want to consider to what extent representative democracy meets the criteria. The requirement of 'personal choice' is met completely by the assumption of methodological individualism developed in Chapter 1, and the requirement, stated on p. 11 that the voters all have equal political power. The model also satisfies the requirement of 'economy'. In order to avoid decision-making costs, the voters can accept a decision rule according to which decisions are taken by a minority.

There are, however, problems in respect of the criterion of 'competence'. Dahl illustrates this criterion by assuming that a surgeon in a hospital or the pilot of an aeroplane knows his job and does not base his decisions on the outcome of an election among the hospital patients and nurses or the aeroplane's passengers and crew. This requirement is met only partly in a representative democracy. In a representative democracy the surgeon and the pilot do indeed decide autonomously how they will do their work, but the patients decide what hospital to enter for an operation and the passengers decide which airline to fly. Translated into political terms: professional politicians can admittedly decide the details of their work autonomously, but whether or not they are competent is judged by persons who are not themselves competent. The only comfort political science and economics have for this dilemma is that we shall have to trust that when the voters take the wrong decisions they will learn from their mistakes.

6

Implementation

6.1 The power of bureaucracy

Bilateral monopoly

For a long time the literature on public administration suggested both that political decisions are made in parliament by elected politicians, including ministers, and that these decisions are implemented by bureaucrats appointed by the administration (Ostrom, 1973). This assumption goes back to Woodrow Wilson (1887) and Max Weber (1922) who regarded bureaucracy as the ideal type of a perfect hierarchy of trained professionals. According to this view the real bureaucrat is not engaged in politics but *administers*, i.e. he administers impartially. The bureaucrat will fulfil his duties *sine ira et studio* (without passion and without partisanship). So he does not do what the politician always has to do, that is, fight. Taking sides, battle, passion – *ira et studium* – these are the essence of politics. The bureaucrat's professional honour lies in his ability at all times to carry out his superior's orders, conscientiously and scrupulously, irrespective of whether his objections to certain policies have been ignored.

Yet, this classic governmental view of bureaucracy must be discarded from an economic viewpoint. This became especially clear more than a decade ago from an analysis of the Soviet-Russian bureaucracy. This bureaucracy had expanded to gigantic proportions so that phenomena which are inherent in every bureaucracy became caricatured and, because of this, became clearly visible. Nove (1962; 1968) and Ames (1965) broke new ground with the unmasking of the totalitarian myth, i.e. the myth that every bureaucrat in Soviet Russia actually does his duty. Williamson (1964), Galbraith (1967) and Niskanen (1971) reached a similar conclusion in respect of the administrations of the Atlantic economies.

Not only do the voters and the politicians have the power to make economic decisions, so do the bureaucrats. In Chapter 1 (p. 9) I defined an individual's power to make economic decisions as his influence in so far as it can be used in accordance with his aims and *is backed by the capacity to apply negative economic sanctions*. Pen (1971, pp. 110–12) explained the last part of this definition by an example in which the power to make economic decisions originates in a situation in which the means required by *A* to realise his aims are more or less at the exclusive disposal of *B*, another individual. Two conditions must therefore be met. First, that for the realisation of this aim *A* should in fact *need* the means controlled by the mighty *B*; second, that *A* can only obtain his requirements via *B*. It is only when *B* exercises more or less complete control over the means that he is able to apply a sanction by withholding these from *A*, thus hindering *A* in the realisation of his aims.

This example gives an insight into the balance of power between politicians and bureaucrats. Only politicians have the right to give orders to their departments and they alone can provide the funds necessary for executing these orders. The departments depend on their budgets which are allotted annually by the cabinet and parliament. On the other hand, the bureaucrats have the exclusive command over professional expertise and various types of information so that the cabinet and parliament are dependent on them for the production of the desired social goods. Niskanen (1971, p. 24) rightly concludes that because politicians and bureaucrats each have a certain degree of monopoly, the exchange relation between them can be termed *bilateral monopoly*.

The limitation of a bureaucracy

The larger the public sector becomes, the less important is the right conferred on the politicians to give orders. After all, a minister's scope of control, i.e. his ability to let his political will penetrate all sections of his department, is limited. The same applies to the scope of control of his leading bureaucrats. The concept of 'scope of control' was divided by J. L. Meij (a Dutch business economist) into 'depth of control' and 'span of control'. 'Depth of control' refers to the number of individuals that can be controlled effectively by one departmental head, 'span of control' refers to the number of hierarchical levels that can be managed.

Graicunas stylised the span of control in a theorem which states that when the number of subordinates increases linearly there is an exponential growth in the number of relations between these subordinates so that it is efficient to have no more than four or five subordinates per civil servant.

The validity of this theorem is no longer held to be absolute, but management consultants accept the conclusion that coordinating activities tend to increase more than in proportion to the increase in the number of subordinates. Ames (1965, p. 240) illustrates this by the example of a planning bureau in which the actual span of control is fifteen persons. A bureaucrat – whose position in the hierarchy is arbitrary – then does the following every month: he receives 5 draft plans from above, he returns 5 counter plans, he receives 5 definite plans back, he writes 5 reports about them; he also sends 5 × 15 = 75 draft plans downwards, receives 75 counterplans, returns 75 definite plans and later receives 75 reports. Both the 'input' and the 'output' of this bureaucrat is only documentary. His time is fully taken up by the multiplication of these documents for despatch downwards and their combination upwards.

Attempts are made in bureaus to avoid the coordinating problems, described by Graicunas and Ames, by increasing the number of hierarchical levels, but then a new problem looms up. At each intermediate level the chance that an order will be changed, either deliberately or accidentally, becomes greater, for it is possible that a subordinate will not understand the order, cannot execute it, or does not wish to execute it. The consequences of this are shown in Table 6.1. A subordinate who, for example, executes 90 per cent of his orders could reasonably be expected to comply with the Weberian model of altruism, but even in a chain of such good souls the result would be that at the fifth level only 59 per cent of the Minister's order would be effective. The combined results of a limited scope of

TABLE 6.1 *Depth of control: an example*

Ministerial orders executed at each level (in %)	Ministerial orders executed (in %) if the Administration has:			
	2 levels	3 levels	4 levels	5 levels
95	90	86	81	77
90	81	73	65	59
80	64	51	41	32
70	49	34	24	17
60	36	21	13	8

Source: Ames, 1965, p. 238

control (both the depth of control and the span of control) can be illustrated arithmetically by means of an exaggerated example. Assuming that: (1) each bureaucrat supervises a maximum of six subordinates; (2) an average of 20 per cent of each bureaucrat's time is spent in being supervised, and the same amount of time is spent by each leading bureaucrat in supervisory activities; and (3) 90 per cent of the activities of a bureaucrat are in accordance with ministerial policy, then it is easy to calculate that in a department numbering about 250 bureaucrats spread over three hierarchical levels, more than 100, i.e. a substantial minority, will be engaged in activities which can be regarded as either neutral towards or in opposition to ministerial policy. Should the activities of each bureaucrat accord for only 75 per cent with ministerial policy, then 170 bureaucrats, i.e. a significant majority, will make either a neutral or an obstructing contribution. This leads Tullock (1965, pp. 149–51) to conclude that a bureaucracy, seen from the standpoint of a politician, is subject to the law of diminishing returns to scale: as the number of bureaucrats increases the effective productivity of the marginal bureaucrat drops and after a certain point this productivity even becomes negative. Five years previously, in 1960, the English writer, C. Northcote Parkinson, reached a similar conclusion. There is a clear limit to a bureaucrat's ability to execute orders in conformity with ministerial intentions.

The homo economicus sovieticus

Even if the power politicians have to control the bureaucracy declines as the number of bureaucrats grows, my definition will allow of decision-making by bureaucrats only if bureaucrats are able to use their power of applying negative sanctions *in conformity with their aims*. This brings me to the essence of the application of the new political economy to the bureaucracy: the aims of the bureaucrats, especially the leading bureaucrats.

All post-Weberian sociologists (Merton, Selznik, Gouldner, Mouzelis, Blau, and Crozier) assume that bureaucrats, too, have their own aims. Empirical economic surveys in the Soviet Union justify the conclusion that this aim is not wholly or even preponderantly altruistic. Even though Soviet courts can inflict the death penalty for 'economic crimes' and official propaganda daily urges solidarity with the Communist Party, Nove (1968, p. 18) has incontrovertibly proved the existence of a *homo economicus sovieticus*. Leading Soviet bureaucrats make the most of the scope they inevitably have to maximise their rewards (promotions and premiums). Nove gives many examples. For instance, a state-owned nail factory is ordered to manufacture nails. This order can be given in terms of weight or volume or a fixed gross income. If the order is in terms of kilogrammes, then the factory will manufacture relatively large and heavy nails because the bureaucrats will wish to execute their order at the least possible cost. If the order is given in terms of quantity, then the factory will concentrate on making small nails for the same reason. If the factory is told to ensure a specific gross income, then it will make the most expensive sort. Another example is to be found in the textile sector. If the firm is told to produce a specific number of metres, the width will be much less than normal. If the order is in terms of square metres, quality will be a secondary consideration. If quality is dictated, costs will be disregarded. A capitalist entrepreneur is guided by market prices, a Soviet bureaucrat by production norms and the related production premiums (Nove, 1968, pp. 179–81).

In Chapter 1 (p. 6) I mentioned that Wiles (1962, p. 1), in his book on the Soviet administration, based his argument on the fact 'that there is such a thing as the logic of institutions . . . *partly* for internal, purely economic reasons inaccessible to the sociologist'. This viewpoint makes the *homo economicus sovieticus* a useful starting point for considering the aims of a Western bureaucracy.

The aims of a bureaucrat

It is more difficult to formulate hypotheses on the aims of leading bureaucrats than on those of entrepreneurs or politicians. In conditions of perfect competition, entrepreneurs are forced to maximise their profits on pain of bankruptcy. As long as political competition is entirely open, politicians must try to gain votes or they will be cast out from the political scene. However, a bureaucracy is not characterised by perfect competition, so that it is not possible to get an unambiguous view of the aims of leading bureaucrats from their environment. As a result, any hypothesis on the aims of a bureaucrat will be somewhat speculative.

A distinction is made between the basic and immediate motives of politicians and by analogy this same distinction can be made to apply to the motives of bureaucrats. Downs (1966, pp. 82–5) systematised the basic motives of bureaucrats. On the one hand he refers to the struggle for power, income, prestige or security; on the other the need for loyalty, the desire to serve the public cause, and the involvement in a specific field of policy. It could be said that the first category of motives is that of the 'careerist', the second those of the 'paternalist'. It is not, however, the basic motivation that is important but the immediate motivation which can be used to explain and predict the behaviour of bureaucrats. Ames, Galbraith, Niskanen and Williamson have attempted to articulate these ideas theoretically by simplifying all the basic motives of both careerists and paternalists into one immediate motive.

Ames (1965, pp. 50–1) based his study of the Soviet bureaucracy completely on the assumption, which he himself considers simple, that all leading bureaucrats aim at the maximum output of goods and services by their factories and departments. Independently of Ames, Galbraith (1967, pp. 166–78) developed this idea further. Galbraith argues that in both the Soviet Union and the West a new élite, the *technostructure*, has become apparent, consisting of technical and managerial specialists of large firms and ministerial departments. This technostructure gives high priority to the increase in the production of goods by firms, and its complement, the increase in the output of services by government departments, because 'expansion of output means expansion of the technostructure itself' (Galbraith, 1967, p. 171). Expansion means more security, greater prestige, a higher income, more power and greater satisfaction.

Niskanen, who was the first economist to construct a mathematical model of bureaucratic behaviour, argues that bureaucrats do not aim at maximising their output of social goods but at maximising their budget. He therefore considers the budget to be an adequate approximation for the utility of leading bureaucrats, including those bureaucrats who have relatively little interest in money and a great concern for public affairs. Even if there are a few bureaucrats prepared to accept a low budget, they will not long survive in an environment of budget maximisation (Niskanen, 1971, pp. 179–81; cf. Breton and Wintrobe, 1975, p. 205).

Under normal conditions, Galbraith's hypothesis (output maximisation) and Niskanen's (budget maximisation) will have identical results, as will be shown later. Williamson's hypothesis (1964; 1974, pp. 29–37) has entirely different results. He examined managerial behaviour within private firms on the assumption that appointed managers have an 'expense preference', especially for appointing new staff who will enable the manager to increase his own salary, security, status, power, or professional ability. At first sight, this hypothesis seems identical to Niskanen's. Yet there is a real difference. Whereas the bureaucrat in Niskanen's model needs a budget to increase his *output*, the manager in Williamson's model needs a budget to increase his *input* (in the form of more staff) even when no extra output results from it. As Niskanen has shown that such an aim will not be met in a bureaucracy which gets its orders from *politicians*, I shall ignore Williamson's hypothesis for the time being, and in the remainder of this chapter I shall therefore assume that the head of a bureau will maximise his output and his budget simultaneously. He does this to realise social and/or private aims.

6.2 Bureaucratic behaviour

Niskanen's model

Niskanen's model (1971, pp. 45–8) is fairly simple. According to him the preference politicians have in respect of a given output of public services can be expressed by means of a 'budget output function'. Any point on this function represents the maximum budget (B) that the politicians, if necessary, would like to spend on a given output (Q). For the sake of convenience Niskanen writes the 'budget output function' as follows:

$$B = aQ - bQ^2 \qquad 0 \leqslant Q \leqslant \frac{a}{2b} \qquad (1)$$

where a and b are positive coefficients. In pp. 32–3 I did not speak of a *budget output* but of a *demand* for social goods. It is not difficult to appreciate the difference between these two concepts. When (as on pp. 31–2) variations in income are ignored, the budgets (B) which politicians would, if necessary, be prepared to supply, coincide with their total benefits. However, demand by individuals depends on their marginal benefits. Thus, the political demand function is a budget output function, expressed in marginal terms, as:

$$V = \frac{dB}{dQ} = a - 2b.Q \qquad (0 \leqslant Q \leqslant \frac{a}{2b}) \qquad (2)$$

The graphs in Figure 6.1 (Niskanen, 1971, p. 26) show Niskanen's budget output curve and the political demand curve. The demand curve is downward-sloping, because politicians put the benefit of marginal social goods at less than that of intra-marginal social goods, so that the amount budgeted for the last unit declines as the number of units increases. As a result the size of the total budget (B) which politicians are prepared to authorise for specific social goods will increase less than proportionately with the level of output.

Figure 6.1 *Total and marginal benefits from the viewpoint of politicians*

B = size of the budget
V = marginal valuation of social goods
Q = level of output of social goods

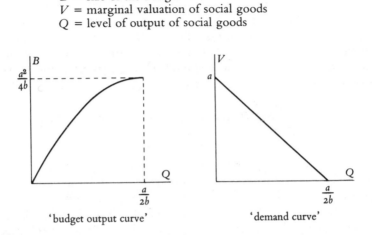

'budget output curve'   'demand curve'

Niskanen makes a clear distinction between the amounts of money which politicians *would like* to budget, if necessary, for a given level of output, and the amounts of money which *must* be paid to provide this output: the costs. According to him, these costs rise more rapidly in every phase than do total costs. However, in my opinion, this assumption, which corresponds to Tullock's assumption of diminishing returns, is not sufficiently well founded. On the whole bureaucrats provide social, not private goods. The cost of producing social goods can indeed rise more than proportionately, but also equally or less than proportionately with output. In Chapter 2 (p. 33) I assumed that the marginal costs of producing a social good are constant, which implies that the total costs rise at the same rate as the production costs. I shall continue to adhere to this assumption in order to avoid less relevant complications in the presentation of Niskanen's argument. My amendment to Niskanen's model thus means that total costs (TC) increase linearly with the level of output:

$$TC = c.Q \qquad (Q \geqslant 0; c > \tfrac{a}{2}) \qquad (3)$$

The coefficient c represents marginal costs. I have assumed that the marginal costs are sufficiently high for the B-curve to cut the TC-curve to the left of the point where $Q = a/2b$ (i.e. the maximum of the B-curve). If the coefficients a, b and c are given, the model has three equations (1, 2 and 3) and four unknowns (B, Q, V and TC). When an objective function is added to the model, the outcome is determined.

The bureaucratic optimum

Niskanen assumed that the objective functions of politicians and bureaucrats differ and this assumption forms the essence of his model. This difference means that the politicians and department heads do not strive to achieve the same ratio between output and real costs. From the point of view of the politicians a programme of social goods is most attractive when output is expanded to the point of maximum difference between its total benefits and its total costs. On the left-hand side of Figure 6.2 it can be seen that the point of the political optimum is where the amount politicians are prepared to budget maximally exceeds what they have to pay. On the right-hand side of Figure 6.2 it can be seen that the political optimum lies where the marginal benefit curve cuts the marginal cost curve. At this point the level of output is $(a - c)/2b$, where the surplus of the politicians is at a maximum.

Figure 6.2 *The bureaucratic optimum*

TC = total costs
MC = marginal costs
B = size of the budget
V = marginal valuation of social goods
Q = level of output of social goods

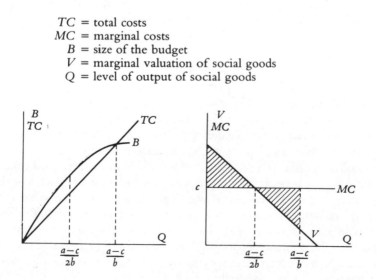

In contrast to the politicians, the utility of the leading bureaucrats is relatively more affected by the benefits than by the costs. For the leading bureaucrats the benefits of social goods, as already noted, consist of a rise in salary, an increase in power and prestige, or satisfaction in their social usefulness. However, the cost of social goods is borne by the voter, in the form of taxation, and, as a result, by the politician in the form of a loss of votes. To some extent the bureaucrats are indifferent to the sacrifices politicians have to make to provide funds. They only need bear in mind one factor, that is that the real costs must be covered by a budget. The objective function of leading bureaucrats thus reads:

$$B_{max} \, (B \geqslant TC) \tag{4}$$

i.e. maximise the available budget finance, subject to the condition that the budget authorised by the politicians will at least equal the costs involved.

The left half of Figure 6.2 shows that the bureaucratic optimum in Niskanen's model is reached when the budget output curve cuts the total costs curve. The political optimum is found where the budget the politicians are prepared to authorise is at a maximum distance from the costs they must pay. The bureaucratic optimum lies where the distance between the amount the politicians want to authorise and the amount they must pay is zero. At this point the bureaucrats have maximised their budget and, as is shown in the figure, also the volume of their output. In this simple model (which ignores the existence of (dis)economies of scale and variations in income) the output desired by the bureaucrats $(a - c)/b$ is twice as large as that desired by the politicians $(a - c)/2b$.

In this model the consequences of a doubling of output is that the political surplus vanishes completely, for the areas of the shaded triangles in the right half of Figure 6.2 are equal. From the viewpoint of the politicians, marginal benefits exceed marginal costs before the point at which $Q = (a - c)/2b$; thereafter marginal costs exceed marginal benefits. The net political benefit of one part of the bureaucratic output is neutralised by the net loss of the other part. For the politicians it would have been ideal if all the social goods of which the marginal output resulted in a loss had never been provided. Leading bureaucrats, however, strive to increase their output far beyond the point of the political optimum. They attempt to neutralise the surpluses which occur in the early phases with the deficits, *until the entire political surplus has completely vanished.*

The compromise between parliament and the administration

The political optimum is determined by the output the politicians demand. The bureaucratic optimum is determined by the output of the leading bureaucrats. As Niskanen characterised the power relations between politicians and bureaucrats as a bilateral monopoly, the outcome of negotiations cannot be determined theoretically. In practice, in his opinion, the bureaucrats generally succeed in getting their own way. Niskanen explains this by saying that politicians are not aware of the real cost function. They know only one point in the cost function, the amount spent on costs at that moment. If this point coincides with the bureaucratic optimum, then every managerial audit will show that the costs do not include any wastage. After all, departments cannot reach the bureaucratic optimum by wasting money. Extravagance would force the cost function upwards and this would lead the politicians to propose cutting down on the output of a variety of social goods. From the bureaucratic point of view the ideal situation can only be attained by extending the production of social goods beyond the point the politicians find desirable. *If there is any inefficiency it must be sought not in the cost of each social good but in the level of output of these goods.*

Thompson (1973) countered this by arguing that when politicians are not informed about the real cost function, they are able to estimate it subjectively, by assuming, as I did, constant marginal costs. Furthermore, they will order the departments to carry out a programme which, based on this assumption, approximates the political equilibrium as closely as possible.

Breton and Wintrobe (1975, pp. 199–202) have drawn attention to the fact that if politicians do not have information on costs they can buy this information. Only in the extreme case of such information being prohibitively expensive do they agree with Niskanen's conclusion. In their view the outcome of negotiations between politicians and bureaucrats will generally be a budget coinciding with the political optimum increased by the amount for which it is uneconomic to have audits.

A note on empirical investigations

In the previous sections three hypotheses of bureaucratic behaviour have been examined. First, Williamson's hypothesis which states that bureaucratic inefficiency is *technical* in nature, i.e. it is shown by a wastage of inputs, especially of staff (pp. 126–7). Second, the hypotheses of Galbraith and Niskanen according to which bureaucratic inefficiency is essentially *economic* and manifests itself in the volume of outputs (p. 126). Third, Thompson's hypothesis, as amended by Breton and Wintrobe, that bureaucratic inefficiency either *does not exist* or it is relatively unimportant (p. 131).

Empirical investigation must determine whether Williamson or Niskanen or Thompson is right. However so far such studies have been fragmentary. The first question studies must answer is whether, independent of possible economic inefficiency, technical inefficiency occurs. Technical inefficiency can be proved by *cost-effectiveness studies*. Such studies regard policy aims as given; they are concerned solely with the costs of achieving these aims. On the basis of a comparative study of the relationship between the costs and the effectiveness of air transport services, fire brigades, sanitation, and the administration of universities, Orzechowski (1977, pp. 248ff) concluded that technical inefficiency *is* found in government bureaucracy, so that Niskanen's prediction that no technical inefficiency will occur in a bureaucracy, is falsified.

The second question investigation must answer is whether economic inefficiency can be found in addition to technical inefficiency. This question can never be answer by cost-effectiveness studies because such studies regard policy aims, i.e. the outputs, as given. In a *cost–benefit analysis* based on welfare economics, policy aims are not given but are unknowns dependent on the economic welfare of the individuals. Such cost–benefit analysis will thus be able to provide a conclusion as to the degree of over-expansion of the bureaucratic output. However, as far as I know, no cost–benefit studies have yet been made to demonstrate in particular the 'Niskanen-effect'.

6.3 Bureaucracy and economic welfare

Contraction or expansion?

The fact that the bureaucratic optimum differs from the political optimum does not necessarily mean that the former differs from the economic welfare optimum. In Section 5.3 I concluded that politicians in a twoparty system who maximise their votes will achieve a Paretian optimum provided that political competition is perfect and that political information is complete. However, in point of fact, the political optimum will differ from the economic welfare optimum because all conditions are rarely met. There are conflicting views on the nature of this difference.

On the strength of what was said in Section 5.3 about it being difficult in a democracy to pursue a policy when the benefits will only become visible in the future, Downs concludes that the public sector of the economy in a democratic system will always be too small, i.e. smaller than the voter would choose *if he were fully informed*. The 'early' Galbraith (1965) reached a similar conclusion; he claimed that the larger firms persuade the consumer, against his own interest, to concentrate on improving his present standard of living. The manipulation of information in advertising upsets the balance between the public and private sectors in Western economies and contrasts private wealth and public poverty ever more sharply.

The left half of Figure 6.3 illustrates the hypotheses of Downs and of Galbraith. The bureaucratic tendency to expand provides a valuable counter-weight to the short-sighted policies of politicians in respect of the size of the budget. In Dahl's terminology (p. 120) the bureaucracy in this model provides the 'competence' which democracy lacks. If and when politicians and bureaucrats are able to negotiate from positions of equal strength, these negotiations could result in an optimum economic welfare.

Figure 6.3 *Budget, total costs and bureaucratic output*

B = size of the budget
TC = total costs
Q = level of output of social goods
w = optimum economic welfare
p = political optimum
b = bureaucratic optimum

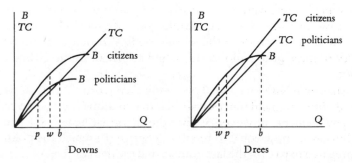

Drees' conclusions, however, are the exact opposite (Drees, 1955, pp. 61–71). In his opinion, the public sector in a democracy is too big, not too small. I have already pointed out (p. 118) that political power, which is the result of the reduction in political competition, means that political parties will avoid conflicts about the *costs* of social goods. In my view this happens only when elections are unlikely to be held, but Drees maintains that it is a constant phenomenon. He claims that the way in which Parliament behaves with respect to the budget depends largely on the dominating role of specialists who play down the costs of the social goods they advocate and concentrate on the benefits which would accrue to the voter.

Drees' hypothesis is depicted on the right-hand side of Figure 6.3. The mere paternalistic behaviour of politicians leads to a higher than optimum budget. The budget will become even higher if the bureaucrats have negotiating power. The positions desired by both politicians and bureaucrats lead away from optimum economic welfare in the same direction. Put differently, the contra-optimal behaviour of politicians and of bureaucrats reinforce each other.

Private firms

One of the most common mistakes in the theory of economic systems is the rejection of a specific structure because it is not an optimum, without considering the extent to which the alternative structure is one. Those who make this mistake can be compared to judges in a beauty contest who, after having seen the first candidate, immediately crown the second. Thus, before discarding bureaucracy as an organisation, it must be compared with its alternatives.

Niskanen (1971, pp. 59–65 and 81–6) and Williamson (1975) compared the methods of coordination of bureaucracy and the market. Niskanen's conclusions especially are relevant to our argument. He says that the Cabinet should get different and competing private firms to produce the social goods – insofar as the indivisibility of these goods allows this – and sell them to the Cabinet at a price.

I shall give Niskanen's analysis in my own words. A private firm is faced with a demand function similar to equation (2) given on p. 127. A new element, however, is that the marginal benefits (V) to the politician are now equal to the market price (P) which the politician is prepared to pay for the last unit, so that the demand equation reads:

$$P = a - 2bQ \qquad (1')$$

The total revenue (R) of the firm, of course, equals the turnover in money terms:

$$R = PQ = aQ - 2bQ^2 \qquad (2')$$

In respect of total costs (TC) I shall, for the sake of presentation, continue with the previous simple assumption:

$$TC = cQ \qquad (3')$$

In respect of the objective function of private firms, Niskanen says that such firms maximise their profits. This is undoubtedly so in conditions of perfect competition. However, in the production of social goods there are often economies of scale which can only be obtained in a monopolistic market (Scitovsky, 1971, p. 373). Perfect competition in the production of social goods is a contradiction in terms and thus runs counter to reality where monopoly, oligopoly or monopolistic competition are more likely. This also means that the assumption that private firms seek to maximise their profits can no longer be maintained. In the first place, the type of market does not force this behaviour. In the second place, large monopolistic firms are bureaucratic, i.e. they are composed of a number of hierarchical departments which may maximise their output. *Niskanen, to quote Nove (1968, p. 22), compares 'muddle with model': he makes the mistake of comparing the reality of a bureaucracy with an imaginary model of the market economy.*

To avoid making the same mistake as Niskanen, I shall assume that a number of aims are possible, not only maximum profits but also maximum output. A firm maximising its profits has as its objective function:

$$(R - TC)_{max} \qquad (4a')$$

A firm maximising its output has as its objective function:

$$Q_{max}; R \geqslant TC) \qquad (4b')$$

The consequences of this model are shown in Figure 6.4 (Scherer, 1970, pp. 400–4). Irrespective of whether a firm is operating under perfect competition, it will, if it is trying to maximise profits, expand its output until its marginal costs equal its marginal revenue. The degree of competition, however, influences the marginal revenue.

In conditions of perfect competition, the firm will regard the market price as given. In this case the market price equals marginal revenue. Individual firms will increase sales until marginal costs equal the market price. Consequently, the point of equilibrium for the whole industry lies where the marginal cost curve cuts the demand curve. Figure 6.4 shows that in perfect competition the point of equilibrium lies at E_o, where $Q = (a - c)/2b$. In a perfect

Figure 6.4 *Industry equilibrium under perfect competition and monopoly*

Q = level of output of social goods
P = price per unit of social goods
D = demand curve
MR = marginal revenue curve
MC = marginal cost curve
m = equilibrium of a profit maximising monopoly
w = optimum economic welfare
b = bureaucratic optimum

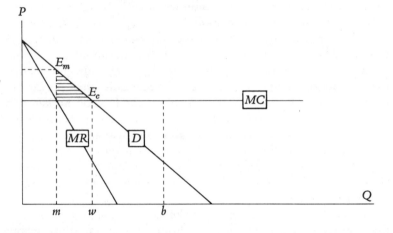

democracy this point is also the point of optimum welfare, because the 'consumer surplus' is at its maximum here.

The outcome is different when competition is restricted. In the extreme case of one supplier (monopoly), the demand curve for the industry will coincide with the revenue curve of the firm. Market price and marginal revenue will no longer coincide so that there is a separate marginal revenue function (MR):

$$MR = \frac{dR}{dQ} = a - 4bQ \qquad (5')$$

It follows from equation (5') that the MR curve must be drawn to the left of the demand curve. The firm will increase its sales until its marginal cost curve cuts its marginal revenue curve. In this case equilibrium is at E_m where $Q = (a - c)/4b$. *A government department in this simplified model wants to produce twice as many social goods as would be the economic welfare optimum, a profit-maximising monopoly would like to produce only half that optimum.* Production by a government department means that the loss of economic welfare (seen partially) would be so large that the whole surplus would vanish. The loss of economic welfare when a private monopoly maximises profits would be less, viz. it would equal the shaded area of the right-angled triangle with E_m and E_c on its hypotenuse.

The loss of economic welfare will be neutralised as soon as the monopoly maximises not its profits but the level of its output, provided that the revenues are sufficient to cover costs. Such a firm will try to find the point at which total costs equal total revenue. In Figure 6.4 this coincides with the optimum economic welfare. A monopoly maximising its output therefore attempts to produce the same quantity as a firm maximising profits in perfect competition.

The conclusion is that the output of private firms in this model equals or is less than the optimum. A private firm achieves its optimum with a smaller loss of economic welfare than a government department. *The cause of this difference lies in the price the politicians (and in fact the voter) must pay for the marginal unit of a social good.* In the model, the firm sells a social good *per unit*. The price the politicians or the voters pay to a firm for the marginal unit in that case is never higher than the marginal benefits. As soon as the marginal costs exceed the marginal benefits, the politicians or the voters will no longer buy the marginal unit. But a government department does not sell a social good per unit but negotiates about the *total* supply of that good. The bureaucrats can give the politicians the choice between all or nothing and thus force them to buy the marginal units at a loss.*

Yet in European countries the implementation of government decisions by private firms is an exception rather than the rule. For a shift from the private to the public sector can also mean a redistribution of income from profits to wages and salaries. On page 37 I recalled that the economic norm contained in the Pareto criterion must always be weighed against an ethical norm, e.g. in respect of income distribution. When production by a private firm satisfying the Paretian optimum is rejected on the grounds of an incomes objective, this is not necessarily irrational.

Self-management by civil servants

In my view the fact that bureaucracy does not work at an optimum can ultimately be explained by two factors: on the one hand the aims

---

* Siccama (1974, p. 421, n. 10) and Orzechowski (1977, p. 132) compare a government department to a price discriminating monopolist. This comparison is not entirely valid. A price discriminating monopolist admittedly appropriates the whole consumer surplus, but it cannot force the consumers to buy marginal units at a loss.

of leading bureaucrats, on the other, the possibility of realising these aims which results from the monopoly position of a department. If remedies are to be found, they must be sought in the removal of these causes. In order to start the discussion on this subject, I launched the idea of self-management by civil servants in 1973 (Van den Doel, 1973, pp. 28–30). Later I found that in the same year Faludi (1973, p. 250), too, had concluded 'that departments formulating programmes, instead of being hierarchically structured, ought to be of a collegiate, self-directing type'. I define the characteristics of self-management by civil servants as follows: (1) all civil servants in a department are equal from an organisational point of view insofar as they choose representatives on a majority vote, who decide on the department's policy and on the appointment of departmental heads; (2) the department is financed exclusively by a budget authorised by the politicians; (3) the politicians negotiate with the departmental representatives about the tasks to be performed for the budget to be provided, and they secure the coordination between the departments; (4) no single department has the exclusive right to provide specific social goods.

If this idea has any value it lies in the fact that the basic characteristics of the model discussed are being extrapolated to the point of absurdity and thus made to reveal their consequences. The fact that the aims of departments are directed at expansion results in the model from the hierarchical structure of a department. The prestige, the salary or the power of the *head* of the department are increased by raising the output or the budget. Irrespective of idealistic considerations, it is also in his own interests to maximise the output or the budget. The pattern of behaviour of the department in the model changes notably if the hierarchical structure is destroyed. Insofar as the civil servants are motivated largely by selfish and not altruistic considerations, the decisions would be made to suit the interests of the lower-ranking rather than of the more senior civil servants. An increase in output (or in the budget) will, however, have different consequences for a lower-ranking civil servant than would have been the case for the person who was previously the head of his department.

An expansion of a department will inevitably mean that the work can no longer be overseen and that there will be a loss of social contacts for lower-ranking civil servants. On the other hand, he can benefit in three respects from expansion. First, the number of supervisors per civil servant will grow so that the freedom to pursue his own policy increases (cf. Tullock, 1965). Moreover, lower-ranking civil servants will have more chances of promotion. Finally, the existing amount of work can be divided among more civil servants.

However, in my opinion, many of the advantages of expansion for lower-ranking civil servants will be lost *in a model of self-management by civil servants*. For a lower-ranking civil servant the gain in policy freedom is wholly compensated by the loss of power because he must share his authority with his colleagues when his section is expanded. In a model of self-management by civil servants, 'promotion' occurs mainly when some civil servants are elected as representatives; it is probable that a civil servant who desires such a 'promotion' will hold up expansion because he fears competition from his new colleagues. When departmental expansion is not expressed in a greater output but in less effort per civil servant, this will be punished in the model of self-management not only by politicians (as described on p. 131) but also by competing departments. 'It may well be that the best of all monopoly profits is a quiet life' (Hicks, quoted in Scitovsky, 1971, p. 418) is precisely what is lost in my self-management model.

The managers appointed by the civil servants will also strive for expansion in a situation of self-management. But within their departments these managers do not possess the monopoly of information about the real cost function. Thus the stimulus to a large departmental expansion will be reduced if it does not disappear altogether.

Vanek (1970, 1975, 1977) examined the economic consequences of self-management within a firm. In a firm with a hierarchical structure, too, the benefits (in this case the financial benefits) of the production process will primarily be of advantage to the managers and the shareholders. As soon as there is a workers' autonomy, however, the benefits will, in Vanek's model, be shared among all the participants in the firm. A number of hypotheses are possible in respect of a workers' collective in such a situation (Vanek, 1975, pp. 30–2). In a wide but vague concept the workers' collective has many aims as regards income, effort, collective consumption, the environment, and community service. In a less wide but more operational concept the members of the workers' collective strive after their own interests, confining themselves largely to matters connected with their income. In this last concept, profit (or output) is not maximised but the profit (or output) per worker (Vanek, 1970, p. 2). However, an increase in profit (or in output) is not possible without an increase in the number of workers. The extra profit must therefore be divided among more workers. This leads Vanek to conclude that a self-managing firm does not tend towards over-expansion: 'perhaps the most important conclusion is a far less danger of gigantism . . . in labor-managed market structures than in just about any other economic regime' (Vanek, 1970, p. 119). By changing some mathematical equations in Vanek's model, Meade (1972, p. 417) has shown that a lessening of the tendency to expand is solely the result of the introduction of a cooperative element in the aims.

The simple mathematical model which was at the basis of my idea about self-management (published in *Acta Politica*, 1974) is put into a graph in Figure 6.5. The horizontal axis does not give the output (Q) but the number of civil servants (L). The total costs (TC) have been split into fixed capital costs (K) and variable wage costs (yL). The bureaucratic optimum and the economic welfare optimum are found in the same way as in Figures 6.2 and 6.3. A new aspect is the optimum of a system of self-management by civil servants, which is achieved within the short run. After self-management has been established, the civil servants no longer strive to maximise the total

Figure 6.5 *Self-management by civil servants without competition*

TC = total costs
K = total capital costs
L = number of civil servants
B = size of the budget
s = optimum self-management without competition
w = optimum economic welfare
b = bureaucratic optimum

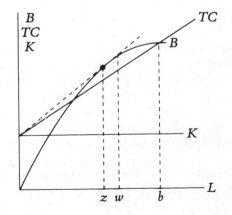

output or the total budget, but to maximise the output or the budget *per civil servant*. If I adopt Vanek's less wide but more operational assumption and moreover *assume that a civil servant is not interested in increasing fixed capital costs*, then the civil servant strives for a maximum value of the quotient $(B - K)/L$ $(B \geqslant TC)$. The graph shows that after the establishment of self-management, the civil servants go from one extreme to another. The excessive increase in the output of the bureaucracy to b is succeeded by an excessive contraction in the output of self-management to z. A consequence of the implied aim is that in the short run the present service will, in a situation of self-management, exploit their monopoly to provide relevant services by preventing new colleagues from joining the civil service corps as is normal in professions, e.g. medicine.

This brings me to the second main problem of a bureaucracy, which is the monopoly position each department has. This monopoly position makes it possible for bureaucrats to make politicians choose between all or nothing, thus forcing them to buy their services at a loss.

Political reformers, faced with the power of a bureaucracy, are always trying to solve this problem by making proposals to sharpen the *external* control of the bureaucracy. The organisation of parliament must be improved, members of parliament should concern themselves more with their departments, ministers should give more guidance, an ombudsman should be appointed, a systematic policy analysis should be financed. In my opinion, these measures will have little effect. At the beginning of this chapter I explained why internal control is limited. The same arguments apply to the limited effectiveness of external control. It is only by stimulating competition between bureaucrats that the *foundations* of bureaucratic power can be demolished.

It is also for this reason that my fourth characteristic of self-management by civil servants is that no single department should have the exclusive right to provide specific social goods. This means that other departments will have *free entry* or that existing departments can take over the tasks of other departments *on condition that the government finances these initiatives*. This condition allows a government to pursue a policy of entry which makes it possible to avoid wastage from duplication.

Under conditions of perfect competition in the administration, politicians are able to confine their executive task to comparing the various plans drawn up by a number of competing departments and choosing the best. In practice, competition will, however, never be perfect because it is difficult to set up a new bureaucratic department.* Yet the possibility that a new department can be set up will work preventively. For fear of a potential competitor the existing departments will be more conducive to the wishes of the politicians. The market for administrative services will no longer be characterised by a bilateral monopoly between the politicians and the bureaucrats, but it will become an asymmetrical structure because one group of politicians will be able to negotiate with competing departments. In the second characteristic of self-management it is laid down that in such a market structure the politicians will be the sole buyer (monopsony) which will give them a strong bargaining position.

Despite the fact that Dahl's three criteria (page 120) were not designed for this purpose, I shall use them to test self-management by civil servants. In the concept of the 'personal choice' of consumers, consumers are taken to include the producers, who may now exchange the Weberian ideal of altruism for the right of choosing their own aims. Concerning the criterion of 'economy', Daalder says, among other things, that self-management by civil servants can result in very high administrative costs of decision-making. Wemelsfelder (1972, p. 6) has shown, however, that a self-managing organisation respects the demands of 'economy' on condition that (elected) representatives make the decisions: in Yugoslavia, which is dominated by workers' councils, not more than 2 per cent of the total working time is used for matters of self-management. In respect of the third criterion, Siccama (1974, p. 420) has remarked that self-management can damage the 'requirement of expert knowledge'. But Dahl himself points out that a departmental committee chosen by the workers (civil servants in this case) will appoint experts on a contract basis, so that 'it is not . . . the criterion of competence . . . that raises problems for self-management' (Dahl, 1970, p. 134).

Despite this optimistic conclusion, the significance of the model of self-management by civil servants is largely heuristic. I aimed to show that economic welfare can be increased by replacing the traditional hierarchical structure in an administration wholly or in part by

---

* In Vanek's model the incentive to establish new departments is weak. Existing departments are not attracted by the opportunity to use their finance to establish new departments, if these funds could otherwise have been used to increase the personal income of the staff. This aspect of Vanek's model is not relevant to self-management by civil servants as in my model a department can be financed solely by politicians.

an '*entente* organisation' such as is sometimes found in hospitals. The model of self-management by civil servants is more revolutionary than the conclusion already drawn by Max Weber (1964, p. 733) and since forgotten, that stimulating *collegiate management* and *administrative competition* coincides with the striving of the public for greater economic and social well-being.

7

The political process

7.1 The political process as a number of production stages

Whereas Chapters 3 to 6 dealt with separate stages of the political process, this chapter will consider the political process as a whole. In a political process the individual voter's demands on, and his support for, the government are converted into government policy, of which, in turn, certain effects are experienced by the individual voter. In my opinion, four methods of decision-making are applied in the course of this process of conversion: negotiation, majority decision, representation, and implementation. I have analysed these four methods of decision-making as independent decision-making models, i.e. as a negotiations *democracy*, a referendum *democracy*, a representative *democracy* and as an implementation *bureaucracy*.

A *negotiations democracy* is the logical basis of every democracy. This basic pattern is split up into the other three decision-making models. In a negotiations democracy each individual is both supplier and demander. Using the method, described by Lindahl, of simultaneous negotiations (*A* negotiates with *B*, *A* and *B* negotiate with *C*, etc.) the individuals reach an agreement. Then they implement this agreement.

A *referendum democracy* specialises in taking binding decisions. Negotiations and decision-making are separated. Decision-making is not by way of a contract but by way of taking enforceable majority decisions.

In a *representative democracy* demanders and suppliers are separated. The demanders are private citizens. The suppliers have an official function, e.g. elected representatives ('politicians') or bureaucrats.

In an *implementation bureaucracy* a function is once again split up. A certain category of suppliers, the bureaucrats, now operate independently in respect of another category of suppliers, the politicians.

As is apparent from the description of the four decision-making models, their listing is not arbitrary. When the political process is compared to a branch of industry producing social goods, then this splitting up can be seen as a form of differentiation in which a new stage has been added to the production stages, which link the primary producer to the final consumer.

The order of these decision-making models is not based on history or chronology but purely on logic. We are not concerned with the relative age of the decision-making model. I do not rule out the possibility that bureaucracy is the oldest method of decision-making, nor that historically there has been integration as well as differentiation. Nor are we concerned with the order in which decisions are actually made. I do not rule out the possibility that there is renewed negotiation after representation has been made and that once again a majority decision is taken.

We are concerned here with a *logical* order, as the comparison with production stages shows. In a political system based on the political power of the voters, which, in principle, is *equal*, only negotiations democracy can function as an independent model. All the other models I discussed necessarily contain elements of the preceding model. For example, a referendum democracy cannot exist unless negotiations have taken place on the voting system and the policy consequences of the outcome of the vote. A representative democracy, in turn, contains elements of a referendum democracy. The voters choose their parliament by a majority of votes; the politicians decide on policy by a majority of votes; all these decisions are binding. The examples of logrolling and of Arrow's paradox of voting, which I discussed in the chapter on referendum democracy, were deliberately taken from representative democracy. Lastly, an implementation bureaucracy cannot exist unless someone gives orders and checks whether these orders have been carried out. In a democratic political system these orders are given not by a dictator but by the masses. It is not possible to compress the multitude of conflicting interests into a single bunch of orders and also to ensure their implementation, unless the voters decide to elect representatives who are specialised in such work.

7.2 The welfare effects of the four decision-making models

In Figure 1.2 (p. 9) the problem of welfare economics examined in this book was described as the question of what organisation of the political system would provide a policy resulting in an optimum economic welfare. Chapters 3 to 6 considered the answer to this question by examining each of the four decision-making models separately. In Figure 7.1 (p. 147) the answer is summarised in a greatly simplified, though conveniently arranged, form.

As has already been noted, a *negotiations democracy* is characterised by freedom of exit and non-commitment. If the individuals negotiate with each other in *small groups* it is not impossible that all individuals will reach their group optimum. However, this does not guarantee that an optimum group welfare will be reached. When negotiations are held on social and quasi-social goods the danger of parasitic behaviour is always present: people will profit from the benefits of social goods but will avoid contributing to their costs. The members of the group can sponge on each other; outsiders can also profit from the group's policy, and vice versa. Thus the small groups will achieve an economic welfare optimum only if two conditions are met. The first condition is that selective stimuli are used to make parasitic behaviour within the group unattractive. The second condition is that the effects of the social goods remain limited to the group which negotiates about them.

When negotiations are held on social and quasi-social goods within *large groups*, it is practically impossible to achieve an economic welfare optimum by way of the institutions of a negotiations democracy. As the members of the group are unable to apply sanctions to each other they will, in normal circumstances, be caught up in a Prisoners' Dilemma: each member of the group is tempted to sponge on the readiness of others to make sacrifices and at the same time he will fear that others will sponge on his generosity. As a result, hardly anyone is prepared to make a sacrifice and the social good will not be produced, not even when everyone very much wants to have it. However, an escape from the dilemma is possible when the group members decide democratically (e.g. by referendum or by electing representatives) to accept coercion, but then the institutions of a negotiations democracy will have served their term.

In a *referendum democracy* group negotiations result in binding majority decisions without the intervention of representatives. The Prisoners' Dilemma of negotiations democracy can now be avoided, but the achievement of an optimum group welfare is threatened by the very high costs of decision-making, which can even mean that the group members leave decision-making to small *oligarchies*. But, also, if the problem of the costs of decision-making is ignored (as was done in Figure 7.1), a majority decision can be afflicted by *cycling* which is a result of Arrow's paradox of voting. If cycling does occur,

Figure 7.1 *Greatly simplified scheme of this book*

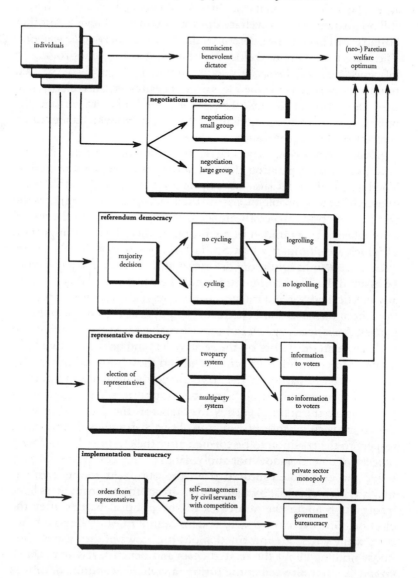

it is impossible to achieve an optimum group policy. Cycling can be avoided by reaching a consensus on the criteria upon which the decision will be based, although it continues to be possible to disagree about the decision itself. But even if cycling is avoided, there is still no guarantee that a welfare optimum will be achieved. Another obstacle will have to be overcome: that of the *tyranny of the majority*. There are two ways to tackle this. The first is to use logrolling to influence political behaviour as is shown in Figure 7.1, so that minorities can exchange their less urgent desires for the realisation of their more urgent desires. The second method is to change the political structure by introducing a voting system which takes more account of the urgent desires of minorities.

A *representative democracy* is characterised by the election of representatives, thus separating the demanders and suppliers of policy. The high costs of decision-making of a referendum democracy are avoided, but new problems arise in their stead. Figure 7.1 ignores the fact that an optimum economic welfare can be realised in the model only when a large number of conditions is met, the most important of which are summarised on pp. 110–12, nos. 1 to 8. But here too, even if these eight conditions are satisfied, an optimum result cannot be assured. Political competition must be so strong that no one has any political power and the voters must have the requisite information about the costs and benefits of the political aims of the political parties. A *multiparty system* cannot satisfy these two requirements. In such a system the parties on the relative left and on the relative right do not compete with each other at all and they compete only partly with the centre parties. They have already achieved an important share of their gains by mobilising their supporters. Also, in a multiparty system the political parties do not, before the elections, provide the voters with reliable information about their political views with respect to the coalition to be formed after the election. In a *twoparty system* this objection does not apply. Both parties compete with each other and each vote captured from the opponent counts twice as much as each vote cast by a supporter. In addition, most voters have information about the strategies of the political parties after the election. However, a twoparty system cannot rule out the possibility that, while voters are informed about the views of the parties, they know nothing about the related costs and benefits. If voters are so *myopic* (i.e. not directed at the future) a welfare economic optimum will not be reached in a twoparty system either.

An *implementation bureaucracy* is characterised by a hierarchy of

bureaucrats, who, though they receive orders from elected representatives, have a certain range of choice in the extent to which they
carry out these orders. They use this range of choice to exploit fully
the preparedness of voters and politicians to accept a certain budget,
if necessary, so that the *output* of the services provided by a bureaucracy in most cases exceeds that which would have been provided by
the preferences of the voters and the politicians. There is, however,
one exception to this conclusion: if the voters are myopic in respect
of the future benefits of social goods but are fully informed about
their future costs, the expansionist tendencies of bureaucracies can
(from the viewpoint of an optimum) provide a valuable counter-
pressure. As it is only possible to speculate on the relevance of this
exception, I assumed in Figure 7.1 that a government bureaucracy
does not reach a welfare optimum and I examined two alternative
methods of implementation on their welfare economic effects.
Firstly, I considered (following Niskanen) *a private firm*. If such a
firm operates within a monopolistic market form and also aims at
maximising profits, we go from one extreme to another: the too
great expansion of services in a government bureaucracy is now
exchanged for a too great contraction in a private monopoly. However, Figure 7.1 ignores the fact that if a monopolistic firm does not
strive after maximum profits but after a maximum output instead, a
Paretian welfare optimum does become possible. The second alternative for an implementation government bureaucracy is described
in Figure 7.1 as *self-management by civil servants*. The idea of this model
is based on Max Weber's forgotten conclusion that the stimulation of
collegiate management and administrative competition can have a
favourable influence on government policy. In this model an
optimum economic welfare can be achieved if, at least, the four
conditions listed on Chapter 6 (p. 138) are met. Some of these
conditions, especially the first one which, in principle, departs from
the hierarchic decision-making method, will give many readers the
impression of Utopia, so that, for the time being, this model can be
given a heuristic value only.

7.3 The public sector: a huge Leviathan?

It was made clear in Chapter 2 that if the production of social goods
and of quasi-social goods is to take place in optimum amounts and at
optimum prices, then an institution is needed which is capable of
adding the demand curves of individuals. In Chapter 2, I demon-

strated that this could be done by an omniscient and benevolent dictator. This conclusion is neither sensational nor relevant. The problem facing all Western economies is whether the methods of decision-making chosen by the voters themselves (a combination of negotiations, majority decisions, representation by politicians, and bureaucratic implementation) are also capable of realising the policy the same voters desire. In Chapter 1, I argued that this problem has become more acute now that over half the national income is in one way or another spent via the public sector.

In order to answer this question I conceived the public sector as that branch of industry producing social goods. However, the rate of expansion of this branch has put that of nearly all other industries in the shade. The problem is now whether the output and the nature of the products of this industry still complies with the wishes of the consumer.

At first sight it would not seem to matter whether expansion occurs in the production of a private firm or of the public sector. In fact there is, of course, one very important difference: the output of private firms is financed by the consumer and is evaluated in the market process, while the output of the public sector is both financed and evaluated by the political process. The study of the effects on economic welfare of the growth of the public sector must therefore be concentrated on a comparison of the market and political processes in all their aspects. This book cannot do more than just mention the most important points of such a comparison.

It is sometimes argued that the political process, of necessity, satisfies individual preferences to a lesser extent than does the market process because the latter is based on competition whereas the former is dominated by a single monopolist: the government. This idea fails to appreciate the fact that the political process, too, can be based on competition between political parties. According to Schumpeter (see page 13) a political democracy is *nothing else* but an institutional arrangement of the decision-making process, in which the politicians acquire the power to decide *by means of a competitive struggle* for the people's vote. Economic theories of the political process build on this Schumpeterian thesis by regarding the political process, too, as a market process in which the voters are the demanders and the politicians and bureaucrats are the suppliers. One of the important conclusions reached with these theories is that under certain ideal conditions there is an *invisible hand*, which brings the self-interest of all individuals via the political process into harmony with one other, so that not only is an optimum (individual) utility achieved but also an optimum economic (group) welfare. In this book these conditions have been discussed a number of times. In order to remove any misunderstanding I shall summarise the most important ones once again:

(1) The voters all have equal political power (p. 11).
(2) When social goods are of value to a large number of individuals, the decisions taken democratically on their production and on the contribution to the costs, are binding (p. 57).
(3) There is a certain consensus among the voters about the criteria on the basis of which the decisions must be taken, even though it is possible to disagree about the decisions themselves (pp. 81–2).
(4) There is perfect competition between the political parties so that they are forced, on pain of liquidation, to strive after the maximisation of their political support by, among other things, implicit logrolling (pp. 115–18).
(5) The voters have been informed about the benefits and costs associated with the politicians' plans for the present and the future (pp. 118–19).
(6) The politicians have sufficient information about the costs of social goods to enable them to force the bureaucrats to carry out their orders scrupulously (p. 131).

This book in no way wants to suggest that Western economies meet these ideal conditions. By the very formulation of these ideal conditions insight can be obtained into the imperfect nature of the political process as it functions in the real world. Of course, it is possible to 'internalise' the external effects of social goods via the political process. But at the same time new external effects can be created. When decisions are not binding, many citizens refuse to contribute to the costs of social goods, even of those they strongly desire. When the decisions bind formally, but not materially, the individual contributions to the costs are evaded or shifted. If the decisions also bind materially, the majority will try to get the minority to pay for the social goods it (the majority) desires. When the politicians are not careerists but paternalists and take decisions within a multiparty system, and when they are not faced with elections for a relatively long period, they will add their own preferences to those of the voters and will then pass these on to the heads of departments, who will, if the hierarchy is not perfectly arranged, distort preferences again. *Without collective action the individuals' utility and economic wel-*

fare cannot achieve an optimum, but even when there is collective action an optimum is rarely achieved under real conditions.

The important question now arises whether in a real situation the actual provision of social goods falls short of or exceeds the welfare economic optimum when the provision is fixed by a political process. An answer to this question can only be given if all stages of the political process are considered in their relation to each other, as I did in Chapter 6 (p. 133) when I integrated the theories of Downs and of Drees with those of Niskanen. After all, it is evident that the effect of each stage of the decision-making process on the size of the public sector will be different. We are concerned with the total result of all the stages. This book argues, for example, that two of the decision-making stages result in too small a public sector, and that two other stages lead to too large a public sector:

(1) *Negotiations* lead to *too small* a public sector because the government does not decide on the size of wages and other incomes (hypothesis of Van den Doel, De Galan and Tinbergen, see pp. 64–72).

(2) *Majority decisions* stimulate the development of *too large* a public sector because the majority makes the minority contribute to the costs of those goods from which it (the majority) alone profits (hypothesis of Buchanan and Tullock, 1965, pp. 131ff).

(3) *Representation*, on the other hand, produces *too small* a public sector because the citizens are informed only about the present costs of social goods and not about their future benefits (hypothesis of Downs and of Galbraith, see p. 133).

(4) Finally, *implementation* leads to *too large* a public sector because leading bureaucrats strive after expansion (hypothesis of Niskanen, see pp. 129–31).

Of course, other hypotheses can also be based on this book. In all cases, however, the size of the public sector is *the result of forces which may conflict in the separate stages of the political process.*

A large part of the literature has ignored this more differentiated approach. With the exception of Downs, most authors argue on a fairly elementary basis that at present the public sector in many democracies is considerably larger than the optimum. Some, following Hobbes (Moss, 1977), even conclude that the public sector is a 'Leviathan' which does not guarantee utility and economic welfare, but threatens them (e.g. Buchanan, 1975, pp. 147ff; Taylor, 1976, pp. 129ff). I have two objections to this conclusion. Firstly, the conclusion is insufficiently argued as I have already tried to show with my analysis of the effects of *separate* stages in decision-making. Secondly, such a conclusion could be seen by a scientific and political forum as a recommendation to reduce the size of the public sector in favour of the private sector. However, Buchanan has said clearly that such a recommendation may be made only when the private sector, in addition to the public sector, has been investigated on its welfare economic aspects.

When comparing the 'public sector' industry and a sector of private industry as *ideals*, the public sector always has the advantage that, in contrast to private industry, it is technically equipped to provide both social and private goods. When comparing the *reality* of the public and private sectors of industry the only possible conclusion is that the two sectors produce under circumstances of unequal power and imperfect competition, so that neither fully makes use of the possibility of meeting the preferences of the consumers. Most market structures in the private sector are characterised by monopolistic conditions, incomplete information, shortsightedness and a slow adjustment to changed circumstances. In democratic decision-making in a large group all the forms of parasitical behaviour discussed above (exploitation by voters of each other, by the majority of minorities, by politicians of citizens, and by bureaucrats of politicians) are possible unless some changes in this democratic process are accepted democratically. Among other things, these changes can concern: the acceptance of government coercion when fixing wages and other incomes, the strengthening of the two-party system, and the stimulation of collegiate management and administrative competition in the 'implementation' power.

As the author of this book, I do not draw the conclusion that these changes *must* be made. I do not regard welfare economics as a normative but as a positive science (see page 37). Everyone is therefore fully within his rights not to accept the application of the welfare economist's conclusion for either ethical or distributional reasons.

The conclusion of this book is only that, under favourable circumstances, the democratic decision-making procedure is able to realise the ideal of an optimum economic welfare to a reasonable extent. Already in 1935, Mannheim, alarmed by the growth of the public sector, pleaded for a *fundamental democratization of society* in order to protect the individual (Mannheim, 1940, p. 44). Summing up, I see no cause to reject this conclusion on economic grounds.

Bibliography

B. Abrahamsson, *Bureaucracy or participation, The logic of organization*, London, 1977.

M. Albrow, *Bureaucracy*, London, 1970.

H. R. Alker, *Mathematics and politics*, Toronto, 1965.

H. R. Alker (ed.), *Mathematical approaches to politics*, Amsterdam etc., 1973.

Ch. M. Allan, *The theory of taxation*, Harmondsworth, 1971.

E. Ames, *Soviet economic processes*, Homewood, 1965.

K. J. Arrow, *Social choice and individual values*, New Haven, 1951; 1963.

K. J. Arrow and T. Scitovsky (eds.), *Readings in welfare economics*, London, 1969.

J. Attali, *Analyse économique de la vie politique*, Paris, 1972.

M. Bacharach, *Economics and the theory of games*, London, 1976.

H. P. Bahrdt, *Industrieburokratie*, Stuttgart, 1958.

B. M. Barry, *Sociologists, economists and democracy*, London, 1970.

R. Bartlett, *Economic foundations of political power*, New York, 1973.

W. J. Baumol, *Welfare economics and the theory of the state*, London, 1952, revised edition, London, 1965.

Business behavior, value and growth, revised edition, New York etc., 1967.

E. L. Berg, 'Decentralisatie in drievoud', Inaugural lecture, Erasmus University, 's Gravenhage, 1975.

A. Bergson, 'A reformulation of certain aspects of welfare economics' (1938), reprinted in: A. Bergson, *Essays in normative economics*, Cambridge (Mass.), 1966, pp. 3–26, and in: *Arrow and Scitovsky*, pp. 7–38.

Th. C. Bergstrom and R. P. Goodman, 'Private demands for public goods', in: *American Economic Review*, 1973.

P. Bernholz, *Grundlagen der Politischen Ökonomie*, Band 1, 2, Tübingen, 1972 and 1975.

R. L. Bish, *The public economy of metropolitan areas*, Chicago, 1971.

D. Black, *The theory of committees and elections*, Cambridge, 1958; 1971.

P. M. Blau, *The dynamics of bureaucracy*, Chicago etc., 1963.

J. C. Blydenburgh, 'The closed rule and the paradox of voting', in: *Journal of Politics*, no. 1, 1971, pp. 57–71.

P. Bohm, *Social efficiency, A concise introduction to welfare economics*, London, 1973.

T. E. Borcherding (ed.), *Budgets and bureaucrats, The sources of government growth*, Durham, 1977.

H. R. Bowen, 'The interpretation of voting in the allocation of economic resources', in: *Arrow and Scitovsky*, pp. 115–32.

S. J. Brams, *Game theory and politics*, New York, 1975.
D. Braybrooke, *Three tests for democracy: Personal rights, human welfare, collective preference*, New York, 1968.
A. Breton, *An economic theory of representative government*, Chicago, 1974.
A. Breton and R. Wintrobe, 'The equilibrium size of a budget maximizing bureau: A note on Niskanen's theory of bureaucracy', in: *Journal of Political Economy*, no. 1, 1975, pp. 195–207.
J. M. Buchanan, *Fiscal theory and political economy*, Chapel Hill, 1960.
Public finance in democratic process, Chapel Hill, 1967.
The demand and supply of public goods, Chicago, 1968.
The limits of liberty: Between anarchy and Leviathan, Chicago, 1975.
Freedom in constitutional contract, London etc., 1978.
J. M. Buchanan and R. T. Tollison (eds.), *Theory of public choice*, Ann Arbor, 1972.
J. M. Buchanan and G. Tullock, *The calculus of consent, Logical foundations of constitutional democracy*, Ann Arbor, 1962; 1965.
J. M. Buchanan and R. E. Wagner, *Democracy in deficit*, New York, 1977.
Ph. M. Burgess and J. A. Robinson, 'Alliances and the theory of collective action: A simulation of coalition processes', in: *Midwest journal of political science*, 1969, pp. 194–218.
J. Burkhead and J. Miner, *Public expenditure*, London etc., 1971.
A. Campbell et al., *The American voter*, New York, 1960.
R. B. Carson (ed.), *Government in the American economy, Conventional and radical studies on the growth of state economic power*, Lexington etc., 1973.
R. L. Carson, *Comparative economic systems*, New York–London, 1973.
M. Crozier, *The bureaucratic phenomenon*, Chicago, 1964.
R. M. Cyert and J. G. March, *A behavioral theory of the firm*, Englewood Cliffs NJ, 1963.
H. Daalder, *Politisering en lijdelijkheid in de nederlandse politiek*, Assen, 1974a.
'De politisering van het bestuur: een nabeschouwing', in: Vereniging voor bestuurskunde (ed.), *Politisering van het openbaar bestuur*, 's Gravenhage, 1974b.
R. A. Dahl, *A preface to democratic theory*, Chicago, 1956.
After the revolution?, Authority in a good society, New Haven etc., 1970.
Polyarchy, New Haven etc., 1971.
R. A. Dahl and E. R. Tufte, *Size and democracy*, Stanford, 1973.
O. A. Davis, M. J. Hinich and P. C. Ordeshook, 'An expository development of a mathematical model of the electoral process', in: *The American Political Science Review*, 1970, pp. 426–48.
J. W. De Beus, 'De onafwendbaarheid van een geleide loonpolitiek', *Economisch Statistische Berichten*, 8 and 15 February 1978.
J.-Ch. De Borda, 'Mémoire sur les élections au scrutin', *Mémoires de l'Académie Royale des Sciences*, Paris, 1781.
A. De Swaan, *Coalition theories and cabinet formations*, Amsterdam–New York, 1973.
A. De Tocqueville, *Democracy in America*, Volume I, 1835; New York, 1948.
M. Dobb, *Welfare economics and the economics of socialism*, Cambridge, 1970.
M. Dole, 'An economic theory of bureaucracy' (mimeographed), Ann Arbor, 1974.

156 *Bibliography*

A. Downs, *An economic theory of democracy*, New York, 1957.
'Why the government budget is too small in a democracy', in: E. S. Phelps (ed.), *Private wants and public needs*, second edition, New York, 1965, pp. 76–95.
Inside bureaucracy, Boston, 1966.
W. Drees, *On the level of government expenditure in the Netherlands after the war*, Leiden, 1955.
Y. Dror, *Public policymaking reexamined*, Scranton, 1968.
D. Easton, *A framework for political analysis*, London, 1965a.
A systems analysis of political life, London, 1965b.
J. E. Ellemers et al., *Macht, machthebbers en machtelozen*, Meppel, 1969.
M. J. Ellman, 'Individual preferences and the market', in: *Economics of planning*, no. 3, 1966, pp. 241–50.
Socialist planning, Cambridge, 1979.
F. Engels, *The origin of the family, private property, and the state*, 1844.
W. Eucken, *Die Grundlagen der Nationalökonomie*, Heidelberg, 1940; 1959.
Grundsätze der Wirtschaftspolitik, Tübingen, 1968.
A. Faludi, *Planning theory*, Oxford, 1973.
R. Farquharson, *Theory of voting*, New Haven, 1969.
B. S. Frey, 'Die ökonomische Theorie der Politik oder die neue politische Ökonomie: Eine Übersicht', in: *Zeitschrift für die gesamte Staatswissenschaften*, 1970a, pp. 1–23.
'Models of perfect competition and pure democracy', in: *Kyklos*, 1970b, pp. 736–55.
Modern political economy, London, 1978.
B. S. Frey und W. Meissner, *Zwei Ansätze der Politischen Ökonomie, Marxismus und ökonomische Theorie der Politik*, Frankfurt am Main, 1974.
B. S. Frey and F. Schneider, 'A politico-economic model of the United Kingdom', in: *The Economic Journal*, June 1978, pp. 243–53.
N. Frohlich and J. A. Oppenheimer, *Modern political economy*, Englewood Cliffs, 1978.
N. Frohlich, J. A. Oppenheimer and O. R. Young, *Political leadership and collective goods*, Princeton, 1971.
N. Frohlich, J. A. Oppenheimer, J. Smith and O. R. Young, 'A test of Downsian voter rationality: 1964 presidential voting', in: *The American Political Science Review*, March 1978, pp. 178–97.
G. Gäfgen, 'Zur Ökonomie der Ideologiebildung', in: H. Sauermann and E.-J. Mestmäcker (eds.), *Wirtschaftsordnung und Staatsverfassung*, Tübingen, 1975, pp. 163–82.
J. K. Galbraith, 'The dependence effect and social balance', in: E. S. Phelps (ed.), *Private wants and public needs*, second edition, New York, 1965, pp. 13–36.
The new industrial state, London, 1967.
Economics and the public purpose, Boston, 1973.
V. P. Gandhi, 'Wagner's law of public expenditure: Do recent cross-section studies confirm it?', in: *Public Finance*, no. 1, 1971, pp. 44–56.
M. Godelier, *Rationality and irrationality in economics*, New York etc., 1972.

T. Grondsma and H. Van den Doel, 'Rationaliteit in het bestuurlijk proces – Een systeembenadering', in: *Bestuurswetenschappen*, May–June 1975, pp. 187–204.

'Enkele betrekkingen tussen inkomensverdeling en demokratie, Een eerste verkenning', *Amsterdams Sociologisch Tijdschrift*, March 1978, pp. 507–17.

B. Guggenberger, 'Okonomie und Politik, Die Neomarxistische Staatsfunktionenlehre', in: *Neue Politische Literatur*, 1974, Heft 4.

F. A. Hayek, *The road to serfdom*, London, 1944.

Individualism and economic order, Chicago, 1948.

The constitution of liberty, Chicago, 1960.

Law, legislation and liberty, Chicago, 1973.

F. A. Hayek (ed.), *Collectivist economic planning*, London, 1935.

J. G. Head, 'Public goods and public policy', in: Ch. K. Rowley (ed.), *Readings in industrial economics*, Volume Two, London, 1972, pp. 66–87.

P. Hennipman, *Economisch motief en economisch principe*, Amsterdam, 1945.

'Pareto optimality: Value judgment or analytical tool?', in: J. S. Cramer et al. (eds.), *Relevance and precision, Essays in honour of P. De Wolff*, Alphen aan den Rijn, 1976, pp. 39–69.

Welvaartstheorie en economische politiek, edited by H. Van den Doel and A. Heertje, Alphen aan den Rijn, 1977 (English translation forthcoming).

Ph. G. Herbst, *Alternatives to hierarchies*, Leiden, 1976.

M. J. Hinich and P. C. Ordeshook, 'Plurality maximization versus vote maximization: A spatial analysis with variable participation', in: *The American Political Science Review*, 1970, pp. 772–91.

F. Hirsch, *Social limits to growth*, London, 1977.

A. O. Hirschman, *Exit, voice and loyalty*, Cambridge (Mass.), 1970.

A. Hoogerwerf, *Politiek in beweging*, Alphen aan den Rijn, 1971.

H. Hotelling, 'Stability in competition', in: *The Economic Journal*, 1929, pp. 41–57.

N. Howard, *Paradoxes of rationality; Theory of metagames and political behaviour*, Cambridge (Mass.), 1971.

R. J. In 't Veld, 'Stemmingen volgens het meerderheidsstelsel', in: *De Economist*, no. 4, 1967, pp. 499–513.

'Stemmenhandel', in: *De Economist*, no. 1, 1969, pp. 24–72.

Meerderheidsstelsel en welvaartstheorie, Leiden, 1975.

G. A. Irwin and J. Thomassen, 'Issue-consensus in a multiparty system: Voters and leaders in the Netherlands', in: *Acta Politica*, October 1975, pp. 389–420.

L. Johansen, *Public economics*, Amsterdam, 1965.

M. Z. Kafoglis, *Welfare economics and subsidy programs*, Gainesville (Florida), 1962.

A. Kapteyn, *A theory of preference formation*, Leiden, 1977.

V. O. Key, *The responsible electorate*, New York, 1966.

E. S. Kirschen (et al.), *Economic policy in our time*, second edition, Part I, Amsterdam, 1968.

J. J. Klant, *Spelregels voor economen*, Leiden, 1972 (English translation forthcoming).

J. A. M. Klaver and J. G. Siccama, 'Integratie van politicologie en economie', in: *Acta Politica*, April 1974, pp. 125–61.

J. Kornai, *Anti-equilibrium*, Amsterdam, 1971.

D. Krech, S. Crutchfield and E. L. Ballachy, *Individual in society*, New York, 1962.

G. Kuypers, *Grondbegrippen van politiek*, Utrecht, 1973.

O. Lange and F. M. Taylor, *On the economic theory of socialism*, New York etc., 1938.

C. J. Lammers, 'De zwanezang van de Leidse senaat', in: *Universiteit en Hogeschool*, Sept. 1973.

H. Leibenstein, *Beyond economic man*, Cambridge (Mass.), 1976.

A. Lijphart, 'De paradox van Condorcet en de Nederlandse parlementaire praktijk', in: *Acta Politica*, April 1975, pp. 188–98.

E. Lindahl, 'Just taxation – A positive solution' (1919), in: *Musgrave and Peacock*, pp. 168–76.

C. E. Lindblom, *The policy-making process*, Englewood Cliffs NJ, 1968. *Politics and markets*, New York, 1977.

I. M. D. Little, *A critique of welfare economics*, 1950; London, 1960.

B. J. Loasby, *Choice, complexity and ignorance*, Cambridge, 1976.

R. D. Luce and H. Raiffa, *Games and decisions*, New York, 1957.

K. Mannheim, *Man and society in an age of reconstruction*, 1935; London, 1940.

J. Marschak and R. Radner, *Economic theory of teams*, New Haven, etc., 1972.

A. Marshall, *Principles of economics*, 1890; eighth edition, London, 1961.

F. M. Marshall, A. M. Cartter and A. G. King, *Labor economics*, Homewood (Ill.), 1976.

K. Marx, *Capital*, 1867; Moscow, 1965–67, Vol. I.

K. Marx and F. Engels, *Manifesto of the Communist Party*, 1848; Moscow (undated).

D. J. Mayston, *The idea of social choice*, London, 1974.

C. B. McGuire and R. Radner (eds.), *Decision and organization*, Amsterdam, 1972.

R. B. McKenzie and G. Tullock, *The new world of economics*, Homewood (Ill.), 1975.

J. E. Meade, 'The theory of labour-managed firms and of profit sharing', in: *Economic Journal*, 1972, pp. 402–28.

A. H. Q. M. Merkies, 'Van prognoses naar programma's', Inaugural lecture, Free University, Amsterdam, 1973.

A. H. Q. M. Merkies and J. Weitenberg, 'A principal component analysis of government expenditure in the Netherlands', in: J. H. P. Paelinck (ed.), *Programming for Europe's collective needs*, Amsterdam, 1970, pp. 99–135.

R. Michels, *Political Parties*, 1911; New York–London, 1962.

J. L. Migué and G. Bélanger, 'Toward a general theory of managerial discretion', in: *Public Choice*, Spring 1974, pp. 27–47.

J. S. Mill, *Considerations on representative government*, London, 1861.

R. Millward, *Public expenditure economics, An introductory application of welfare economics*, London, 1971.

E. J. Mishan, *Welfare economics, Ten introductory essays*, New York, 1969. *Cost–benefit analysis*, London, 1971; second edition, 1975.

W. C. Mitchell, 'The Shape of Political Theory to come: From political sociology to political economy', in: *The American Behavioral Scientist*, Nov.–Dec. 1967, pp. 8–37.

'Review of W. Niskanen: Bureaucracy and representative government', in: *American Political Science Review*, Dec. 1974, pp. 1775–7.

B. M. Mitnick, 'The theory of agency. The policing paradox and regulatory behaviour', in: *Public Choice*, Winter 1975, pp. 27–42.

J. M. Montias, *The structure of economic systems*, New Haven etc., 1976.

L. S. Moss, 'Some public-choice aspects of Hobbes's political thought', in: *History of Political Economy*, Summer 1977, pp. 256–72.

D. C. Mueller, 'Public choice: A survey', in: *Journal of Economic Literature*, June 1976, pp. 395–433.

Public choice, Cambridge, 1979.

D. C. Mueller, G. C. Philpotts and J. Vanek, 'The social gains from exchanging votes: A simulation approach', in: *Public Choice*, Fall 1972, pp. 55–79.

R. A. Musgrave, *The theory of public finance, A study in political economy*, New York etc., 1959.

R. A. Musgrave and A. T. Peacock, *Classics in the theory of public finance*, New York, 1958; 1967.

R. A. Musgrave and P. B. Musgrave, *Public finance in theory and practice*, second edition, New York etc., 1976.

G. Myrdal, *The political element in the development of economic theory*, London, 1953.

S. K. Nath, *A reappraisal of welfare economics*, London, 1969.

R. G. Niemi and W. H. Riker, 'The choice of voting systems', in: *Scientific American*, June 1976, pp. 21–7.

W. A. Niskanen, *Bureaucracy and representative government*, Chicago etc., 1971.

W. A. Niskanen, D. Houghton, M. Kogan, N. Ridley and Ian Senior, *Bureaucracy: Servant or Master?*, London, 1973.

G. P. Noordzij, 'Het politieke systeem', in: Van Schendelen, 1976, pp. 13–35.

A. Nove, *The Soviet economy*, 1962; third edition, London, 1968.

The Soviet economic system, London, 1977.

J. O'Connor, *The fiscal crisis of the state*, New York, 1973.

M. Olson, *The logic of collective action, Public goods and the theory of groups*, Cambridge (Mass.), 1965; second edition, 1971.

M. Olson and R. Zeckhauser, 'An economic theory of alliances', 1968, in: *Russet*, pp. 25–50.

P. C. Ordeshook, 'The spatial theory of elections: A review and a critique', in: Ian Budge et al. (eds.), *Party identification and beyond*, London 1976, pp. 285–314.

W. Orzechowski, 'Economic models of bureaucracy: Survey, extensions, and evidence', in: *Borcherding* (ed.), 1977, pp. 229–59.

V. Ostrom, *The intellectual crisis in American public administration*, Alabama, 1973.

A. N. Page (ed.), *Utility theory, A book of readings*, New York etc., 1968.

M. Palmer, L. Stern and Ch. Gaile, *The interdisciplinary study of politics*, New York, 1974.

V. Pareto, *Manual of political economy*, 1906; Paris 1909; New York, 1971.

J. Pen, *Harmony and conflict in modern society*, London–New York, 1966.
'Bilateral Monopoly, Bargaining and the concept of economic power', in: K. W. Rothschild (ed.), *Power in economics*, Harmondsworth, 1971, pp. 97–115.

A. C. Pigou, *The economics of welfare*, 1920; fourth edition, London, 1946.
Study in public finance, third edition, London, 1947.

C. M. Price, *Welfare economics in theory and practice*, London, 1977.

F. L. Pryor, *Public expenditures in communist and capitalist nations*, London, 1968.
Property and industrial organization in communist and capitalist nations, Bloomington etc., 1973.

A. Rapoport, 'Prisoners' Dilemma – Recollections and observations', in: A. Rapoport (ed.), *Gametheory as a theory of conflict resolution*, Dordrecht, 1974.

A. Rapoport and A. M. Chammah, *Prisoners' Dilemma*, Ann Arbor, 1965.

M. Rheinstein (ed.), *Max Weber on law in economy and society*, New York, 1954.

W. H. Riker and P. C. Ordeshook, 'A theory of the calculus of voting', in: *The American Political Science Review*, no. 1, 1968, pp. 25–42.
An introduction to positive political theory, Englewood Cliffs N.J., 1973.

L. Robbins, *An essay on the nature and significance of economic science*, London, 1935.

D. Robertson, *A theory of party competition*, London etc., 1976.

W. Röpke, *Die Lehre von der Wirtschaft*, Zürich, 1954.

S. A. Ross, 'The economic theory of agency: The principal's problem', in: *American Economic Review*, May 1973, pp. 134–9.

J. Rothenberg, *The measurement of social welfare*, Englewood Cliffs NJ, 1961.

C. K. Rowley and A. T. Peacock, *Welfare economics, A liberal restatement*, London, 1975.

B. M. Russet (ed.), *Economic theories of international politics*, Chicago, 1968.

L. M. Salamon and J. J. Siegfried, 'Economic power and political influence', in: *The American Political Science Review*, Sept. 1977, pp. 1026–43.

P. A. Samuelson, 'The pure theory of public expenditure', 1954; reprinted in: *Arrow and Scitovsky*, pp. 179–82.
'Towards a pure theory of public expenditure', in: B. S. Sahni, *Public expenditure analysis*, Rotterdam, 1972, pp. 74–88.

F. M. Scherer, *Industrial market structure and economic performance*, Chicago, 1970.

L. R. Schmidt, *The new political economy: The public use of the private sector*, London, 1975.

O. Schmidt, 'The abolition of compulsory voting in the Netherlands: Some empirical findings', *Paper European Consortium for Political Research*, Strasbourg, 1974.

O. Schmidt and R. J. van der Veen, 'Rationaliteit en moraal: Het prisoners' dilemma', in: *Acta Politica*, April 1976, pp. 178–205.

E. F. Schumacher, *Small is beautiful*, London 1973.

Bibliography   161

J. A. Schumpeter, *Capitalism, socialism and democracy*, fourth edition, London, 1954.

T. Scitovsky, 'Two concepts of external economies', in: *Arrow and Scitovsky*, 1969, pp. 242–52.

Welfare and competition, revised edition, London, 1971.

A. K. Sen, *Collective choice and social welfare*, San Francisco, 1970.

'Choice, Orderings and Morality', in: S. Körner (ed.), *Practical Reason*, New Haven, 1974, pp. 54–67.

W. R. Shaffer, *Computer simulations of voting behavior*, New York etc., 1972.

W. G. Shepherd, *Market power and economic welfare, An introduction*, New York, 1970.

K. A. Shepsle, 'Theories of collective choice', in: *Political Science Annual*, 1974, pp. 1–87.

M. Shubik, 'A two party system, general equilibrium and the voters' paradox', in: *Zeitschrift für Nationalökonomie*, 1968, pp. 341–54.

J. G. Siccama, 'Ekonomie en demokratie in het staatsbestuur: Een kritische reaktie', in: *Acta Politica*, Oct. 1974, pp. 413–32.

H. A. Simon, *Models of man*, New York, 1957.

Administrative behaviour, 1957; second edition, New York, 1965.

'Theories of bounded rationality', in: *McGuire and Radner*, pp. 161–76.

M. Sproule-Jones and K. D. Hart, 'A public choice model of political participation', in: *Canadian Journal of Political Science*, Jan. 1973, pp. 175–94.

R. S. Sterne, A. Rabushka and H. A. Scott, 'Serving the elderly? An illustration of the Niskanen effect' in: *Public Choice*, Fall 1972, pp. 81–90.

T. A. Stevers, 'Welke factoren bepalen de veranderingen in het niveau en de structuur van de belastingen in de 19e en 20e eeuw?', in: *Smeetsbundel*, Deventer, 1967.

'Een economische analyse van het demokratisch proces', in: *Welvaart en demokratie*, Tilburg, 1968, pp. 37–70.

G. J. Stigler, *The citizen and the state*, Chicago, 1975.

G. J. Stigler et al., 'Micropolitics and macroeconomics', in: *American Economic Review*, May 1973, pp. 160–79.

P. M. Sweezy, *The theory of capitalist development*, New York, 1968.

M. Taylor, 'Review Article: Mathematical political theory', in: *British Journal of Political Science*, 1971, pp. 339–82.

Anarchy and cooperation, London, 1976.

H. A. A. M. Thoben, 'Een economische theorie van ontwikkelingshulp', in: *Economie*, April 1971, pp. 326–33.

E. A. Thompson, 'Review of W. A. Niskanen: Bureaucracy and representative government', in: *Journal of Economic Literature*, Sept. 1973, pp. 950–3.

J. Tinbergen, 'The theory of the optimum regime', in: L. H. Klaassen (ed.), *Jan Tinbergen selected papers*, Amsterdam, 1959, pp. 264–304.

'The significance of welfare economics for socialism', in: *On political economy and econometrics*, Essays in honour of Oscar Lange, Warsaw, 1964.

'De toekomstige sociale orde en onze beweging', in: *Socialisme en Democratie*, November 1965, pp. 728–43.

J. Tinbergen – *Cont.*
  'Gegenwärtige Probleme der Theorie des volkswirtschaftlichen Wohl-
  stands', in: *Statistische Hefte*, Heft 3, 1967.
  Income distribution, Analysis and policies, Amsterdam, 1975.
  Income differences: Recent research, Amsterdam, 1976.
G. Tullock, *The politics of bureaucracy*, Washington, 1965.
  Toward a mathematics of politics, Ann Arbor, 1967.
  Private wants, public means, New York etc., 1970.
  The logic of the law, New York etc., 1971.
  The vote motive, Hobart Paperback no. 9, London, 1976.
G. Tullock (ed.), *Explorations in the theory of anarchy*, Blacksburg, 1972.
H. Van den Doel, *Konvergentie en evolutie, De konvergentietheorie van Tin-
  bergen en de evolutie van ekonomische ordes in Oost en West*, Assen, 1971.
  'Ekonomie en demokratie in het staatsbestuur', Inaugural lecture Nij-
  megen–Amsterdam, 1973.
  'Baten en offers in het bestuurlijk systeem', in: *Acta Politica*, Oct. 1974, pp.
  423–31.
  'De makro-politieke paradox van Arrow's nachts in het parlement', in:
  Acta Politica, April 1975a, pp. 199–204.
  Demokratie en welvaartstheorie, Alphen aan den Rijn, 1975b; second edition,
  Alphen aan den Rijn, 1978.
  'Carry out the revolution and increase production! The evolution of the
  Chinese economic order to an optimum', in: *De Economist*, no. 2, 1977,
  pp. 211–37.
H. Van den Doel, C. de Galan and J. Tinbergen, 'Pleidooi voor een geleide
  loonpolitiek', I en II, in: *Economisch Statistische Berichten*, 17 March and
  1 September 1976, pp. 264–8 and 828–31.
J. A. A. Van Doorn, 'Inleiding tot Robert Michels en zijn thematiek', in:
  R. Michels, *Democratie en organisatie*, Rotterdam, 1969.
B. M. S. Van Praag, *Individual welfare functions and consumer behavior*, Am-
  sterdam, 1968.
  'The welfare function of income in Belgium: An empirical investigation',
  in: *European Economic Review*, 1971, pp. 337–69.
B. M. S. Van Praag and A. Kapteyn, 'Further evidence on the individual
  welfare function of income: An empirical investigation in the Nether-
  lands', in: *European Economic Review*, 1973, pp. 33–62.
M. Van Schendelen (ed.), *Kernthema's van de politicologie*, Meppel, 1976.
E. Van Thijn, 'Van partijen naar stembusaccoorden', in: *Partijvernieuwing*,
  Amsterdam, 1967.
J. Vanek, *The general theory of labor-managed economies*, Ithaca etc., 1970.
  The labor-managed economy, Ithaca etc., 1977.
J. Vanek, (ed.), *Self-management: Economic liberation of man*, Harmondsworth,
  1975.
T. Veblen, *The place of science in modern civilisation, and other essays*, 1919.
L. Von Mises, *Bureaucracy*, London, 1945.
J. Von Neumann and O. Morgenstern, *Theory of games and economic
  behavior*, 1944; third edition 1953; eleventh printing, Princeton, 1974.
L. L. Wade and R. L. Curry, *A logic of public policy, Aspects of political economy*,
  Belmont, 1970.

D. Waldo, 'Developments in public administration', in: *The annals of the American Academy of Political and Social Science*, November 1972, pp. 217–45.

M. Weber, *Wirtschaft und Gesellschaft*, Berlin, 1922; Studienausgabe, Köln–Berlin, 1964.

J. Wemelsfelder, 'Arbeiderszelfbestuur in de Joegoslavische industrie', supplement to *Economisch Statistische Berichten*, 15 March 1972.

K. Wicksell, 'A new principle of just taxation' (1896), in: Musgrave and Peacock, pp. 72–118.

H. L. Wilensky, *The welfare state and equality*, Berkeley, 1975.

P. J. D. Wiles, *The political economy of communism*, Oxford, 1962.

Economic institutions compared, Oxford, 1977.

O. E. Williamson, *The economics of discretionary behavior: Managerial objectives in a theory of the firm*, dissertation 1964; second edition, London, 1974.

'Markets and hierarchies: Some elementary considerations', in: *American Economic Review*, May 1973, pp. 316–34.

Markets and hierarchies: Analysis and antitrust implications, New York, 1975.

W. Wilson, 'The study of administration', in: L. C. Gawthrop (ed.), *The administrative process and democratic theory*, Boston, 1970, pp. 77–85.

D. M. Winch, *Analytical welfare economics*, Harmondsworth, 1971.

D. A. Wittman, 'Parties as utility maximizers', in: *The American Political Science Review*, 1973, pp. 490–8.

C. Wright Mills, *White collar*, New York, 1951.

Index of subjects

administration, 121, 122–4, 131
aims
  of civil servants, 125–7
  consistent, 20–1
  economic, 19
  of groups, 42–3
  of individuals, 18–19
  measurement of, 23–5
  policy, 97–8, 103, 108, 110
alienation, 99–100, 104, 112
altruism, 59–60, 69, 123, 138
anarchy, 12, 60–1
apathy
  negative, 51, 56, 100
  positive, 51, 56, 100
Arrow paradox, 78–80, 85, 146–7
  empirical examples of, 82–4
  and single-peakedness, 80–2
  and value-restrictedness, 81–2, 84
    (*see also* consensus)
  and voting systems, 90
assumptions
  of the economic theory of political decision-making, 5–6, 18–25, 42
  of the models, 67–72, 108, 110, 112, 117–19, 135, 151
assurance game, 59–60

behaviour
  bureaucratic, 127–30
  electoral, 99–100
  political, 87, 96, 104–8, 116
  strategic, 74–5, 75, 92, 118
budget, 14, 122, 126–7
  maximisation of, 126–7, 130, 132, 141
budget output function, 127–8
bureaucracy
  aims of, 125–7, 130, 135, 139–41
  behaviour of, 129–32
  definition of, 11

  development of the concept of, 13–14
  economic theory of, 126, 127–30
  and economic welfare, 132–4, 148–9
  external view of, 13–14
  in firms, 14, 137
  as a hierarchy, 13–14, 122–3
  internal view of, 14, 77
  as a method to coordinate, 11, 13
  in a political party, 14, 77
  span of control of, 122–3
  as a stage in the political process, 16–17, 144–5
  Weber's concept of, 13, 121

cabinet formations, 79, 106–7, 148
candidates, *see* politicians
cardinal method, *see* measuring scale
careerists, 103, 117, 126
centralisation
  definition of, 9–10
  and democracy, 61–2
  of power by the government, 1–2, 61
centre, political, 79, 99, 106, 116
civil servants
  aims of, 125–7, 130, 135, 139–41
  self-management by, 137–43, 147, 149
  span of control of, 122–3
class
  Marx's view on, 42–3
  Olson's view on, 43–4
  Wright Mills' view on, 43–4
coalitions, 47, 64, 87 90, 106, 115–16, 118, 148
coercion
  democratic, 57, 61, 67, 68–72, 146, 151
  effectiveness of, 71
  external, 9, 80, 122, 137
collective action, 40, 44, 53–6, 151–2

collective welfare, *see* economic welfare
collegiate management, 138, 143
command economy, 10, 13–14, 122–4
common interest, 42, 55, 65 (*see also* consensus)
communication, 10, 123
compensation tests, 37–8, 87
competition, 13, 103–5, 109–12, 117–18, 132, 134, 141–3, 148–51, 153
complexity, 22
concentration
  definition of, 9–10
  and democracy, 12, 58–9
  and the structure of an economy, 9
concerted action, *see* negotiations democracy
connectedness, 20
consensus, 99, 148, 151 (*see also* common interest)
consistency
  collective, 79–82, 146–8
  definition of, 20
  -index, 21
  individual, 20, 42, 97, 112
  of political parties, 106, 114
consumer surplus
  definition of, 31–2
  of a social good, 31–2, 39–40, 136
consumption
  exclusion from, 26–9
  external effects of, 25, 27–8
  of social goods, 26
  and utility, 18–20
contests, 78–80, 86, 90
continuum, running from left to right, 97–9, 100–1
convergence
  complete, 107–8, 110–11
  partial, 104–5
cooperation, 45, 50, 58–61
coordination, 9–11, 13, 122–4
corporate state, 68 (*see also* trade unions)
costs
  information about, 118, 131–3
  of scarce goods, 2–3
  of social goods, 31, 128–35, 151
culture, *see* political culture

Dahl criterion, 119–20, 133, 142
De Borda method, 90–3
decision-making costs, 75, 78, 94, 120, 142, 146
decision rule, 20, 22, 36–8, 76

decisions, binding, 4, 57, 61–2, 67, 73, 146, 151
demand
  for a private good, 31–2, 32–3
  for a social good, 32–3, 46, 128, 133, 136, 140
democracy
  and competition, 13, 103, 105, 117–18, 150
  and consensus, 12, 81–2
  and decentralisation, 12, 61–2
  and deconcentration, 12, 58–9
  definition of, 11
  development of the concept of, 13–14
  and economic welfare, 113–20, 145–9
  in firms, 116, 139–41, 142–3
  and information, 118–20
  and majority, 12–13, 73, 85, 93
  as a method to coordinate, 11
  and the neo-democrats, 52, 153
  and the political process, 15–7, 144–5
  and the public sector, 131, 149–53
  and rationality, 41, 78–80, 118–20
  Schumpeter's definition of, 13, 103, 117, 150
  (*see also* negotiations democracy, referendum democracy, representative democracy)
democratic acceptance of coercion, 57, 61, 67, 68–72, 146, 151
dictator, an omniscient and benevolent, 38–9, 114, 116, 147, 150
distribution of income, 26, 37, 65–6, 72, 74, 96, 137

economic order
  as concerted action, 41
  definition of, 8, 9
  optimum, 8, 134
  (*see also* command economy, market economy)
economic power, 9, 117, 122, 151, 153
economic theory of political decision-making
  assumptions of, 6–7, 18–25, 42
  definition of, 5–6, 13
  empirical tests of, 5, 62–4, 82–4, 97, 100–2, 109–10, 131–2
  as integration of economics and political science, ix, 5
  and political process, 16–17, 144–5
  themes of, 5–6

economic theory—*Contd.*
  and welfare economics, ix, 7–8,
    145–9
  (see also *new political economy*)
economic welfare
  definition of, 19
  as an economic end, 35–6
  and implementation bureaucracy,
    132–43, 147–9
  and negotiations democracy, 50–62,
    146–7
  as a neutral criterion, 36–8, 74
  and the political process, 147, 149–53
  and referendum democracy, 85–93,
    146–8
  and representative democracy,
    113–20, 147–8
  and social goods, 38–40
  (see also neo-Paretian criterion, Pa-
    reto criterion, welfare economics)
economics
  definition of, 2
  institutional, 4, 6, 8
  theoretical shortcomings of, 3–4
effectiveness
  of bureaucracy, 122–3
  of coercion, 71
  of democratic control, 141
effects of policy, 15, 16, 144
efficiency
  economic, 132
  technical, 126–7, 131, 131–2
  (see also economic welfare)
elections, 117, 119
empirical investigation, 6, 62–4, 100–2,
    109–10, 131–2
employment, 36, 64–8
ethics, ix, 34, 37, 71, 74, 94, 137, 153
  (see also morality)
exchange, 44–7
  economy, 10–11, 135 (see also log-
    rolling)
expert knowledge, 120, 122, 142 (see
    also information)
exploitation 56, 152–3 (see also power)
external effects
  definition of, 27
  of democracy, 75, 151–2
  negative and positive, 28
  of social goods, 27–9
extremism, 79, 81–2, 100, 104–5

firms, 134–7, 139, 149
full employment, see employment

future, behaviour directed at, 60–1,
    119, 148–9

games
  nonzero-sum, 48–50, 59–60, 64, 90,
    118
  theory of, 48–9
  zero-sum, 48, 118
Gossen, laws of, 30, 31
government
  coercion by, 61–2, 67–72
  definition of, 61–2
  expenditure by, 1–3, 36, 61
  policy of, 5–6, 94–5, 103, 121
  policy horizon of, 119
  responsibility of, 6
  as a unitary being, 3–4, 6
groups
  definition of, 42
  with freedom of exit and without
    commitment, 41, 61, 73, 146,
    151
  small and large, 47, 58–9, 146–7
  welfare and wealth of, 8

homo economicus, 21
homo economicus sovieticus, 124–5

ideal types
  and real types, 10, 74, 119, 121, 135,
    153
ideology
  as a cloak for self-interest, 43, 63,
    71–2
  mobility of, 104–6, 107–8, 110,
    112–13, 116
  neo-democratic, 52, 153
implementation
  as a stage of the political process, 16,
    121, 144, 148–9, 152
implementation bureaucracy
  behaviour of, 129–31
  definition of, 13–14, 16–17, 144
  and economic welfare, 132–43,
    147–9
  (see also bureaucracy)
income
  definition of, 19
  distribution of, 26, 37, 65–6, 72, 74,
    96, 137
  participation and, 95–6
  self-management and, 139
  utility and, 25, 35
incomes policy, 26, 67, 71–2, 95
indifference, 99–100, 112, 117

individualism, methodological, 6–7, 153
indivisibility, 26–8, 135
information, 22, 69, 74, 101, 112, 118–20, 131, 132–4, 139, 147–8, 151
institutions, 4, 6, 8, 40, 41, 125, 144–5
intensity of preferences, 34, 75, 85–7, 115–16, 148
international aid, 63–4
interpersonal comparison of utility, 33–5
interpersonal evaluation of utility, 34, 91, 94
interval scale, *see* measuring scale
intransitivity, *see* transitivity
isomorphism, structural, 6

labour-managed firm, 139–41, 142–3
level of aspirations, 22–3, 25
Leviathan, monster, 149, 152
logrolling, 87–90, 115–16, 148, 151

macro-political paradox, *see* Arrow paradox
majority
  consistency of, 78–84
  and economic welfare, 85–93, 115, 146, 148, 151–2
  qualified, 75–7
  simple, 75, 104
  tepid, 86–7, 115
  tyranny of, 93, 148
  and utility, 73–8
  (*see also* referendum democracy)
majority decision
  as a stage of the political process, 16, 73, 144, 150, 152
manipulation, 92–3, 133
marginal costs and benefits, 31, 38–40, 118, 127–9, 134, 136
market
  and bureaucracy, 10–11, 127–32
  and democracy, 10–11, 94–5, 149–53
  economy, 10–11, 135
  model of a political, 149–53
  (*see also* competition, exchange)
market economy, 10–11, 135
Marxist
  analysis of collective action, 52, 56
  concept of a class, 42–3
  concept of democracy, 11
mathematics, *see* models
maximisation, 21–3

measuring
  economic welfare, 33–5
  interview method of, 23
  revealed preference method of, 23
  utility, 23–5
measuring scale
  cardinal, 24, 85–6
  interval, 23–5
  ordinal, 23–4, 36, 49, 85
  ratio, 24, 34–5
merit goods, *see* paternalism
minority
  external costs to, 75–6, 93
  and oligarchy, 77–8
  passionate, 85–90, 93, 115
  (*see also* majority)
mobility, *see* ideology
models
  assumptions of, 11, 67–72, 108, 110, 112, 117–19, 138, 151
  economic, 5, 14–17, 76, 79–80, 97–102, 104–6, 107–8, 121–30, 134–43
monism, 3, 6
monopoly
  bilateral, 121–2, 131, 142
  of bureaucrats, 131, 134, 138, 141–2
  of the government, 150
  of politicians, 104–5
  of private firms, 134–7, 149, 153
  (*see also* competition)
morality, 59–60 (*see also* ethics)
motivation
  basic and immediate, 103–4, 125–7
multiparty system, 104–6, 148

NATO, 41, 62–3
negotiations
  and bureaucracy, 132–4, 138
  and economic welfare, 50–62, 146–7
  and the prisoners' dilemma, 47–50
  and social goods, 53–6
  as a stage of the political process, 15–16, 41, 61, 144, 146–7, 152
negotiations democracy
  behaviour of, 47–56
  definition of, 16, 41, 144
  and economic welfare, 50–62, 146–7
  in practice, 62–72
neo-Paretian criterion
  application of, 74, 87, 90, 115–16, 132–42
  definition of, 37
  (*see also* Pareto criterion)

new political economy
  assumptions of, 6–7, 18–25, 42
  definition of, 5–6, 13
  empirical tests of, 5, 62–4, 82–4, 97,
    100–2, 109–10, 131–2
  as integration of economics and
    political science, ix, 5
  themes of, 5–6
  and welfare economics, ix, 7–8,
    145–9, 150–1

objective function, 19–20, 25, 27, 36,
    114, 130, 135, 141
oligarchy
  economic explanation of, 77–8,
    146
  iron law of, 77–8
oligopoly, 47, 58, 118
optimum
  bureaucratic, 129–33, 136, 140
  decision rule, 75–7
  economic policy, 73–5, 103
  economic welfare, 35–6, 38–40, 133,
    136, 140, 145–9, 151–2
  electoral, 103, 105, 108
  location, 104, 108
  Paretian, *see* Pareto criterion
  participation, 52, 96
  political, 98, 100, 129–33
  of a private firm, 135–7
  regime, 8
  self-management, 140
  size of the public sector, 39–40,
    149–53
  utility, 30–2, 76, 98, 100, 151
ordinal, *see* measuring scale
organisation
  of bureaucracy, 7, 122–4
  characteristics of, 9–10
  and democracy, 7
  of the economy, 8–10
  and leadership, 77–8
  optimum, 8–9
  of the political process, 144–5
  of the public sector, 8, 11
  of self-management, 137–42
  structure of an, 9–10
other regarding game, 59–60, 69
outcome matrix, 49, 54, 66

parasitic behaviour, 51–6, 146, 153
Pareto, *see* Pareto criterion, unanimity
  rule, welfare economics

Pareto criterion
  application of, 49–50, 52, 54, 60, 61,
    74, 79, 90, 113–15, 132
  definition of, 36
  and income distribution, 37, 74, 137
  practical objections to, 37–8, 74
  and unanimity rule, 73–4
  as a value judgment, 37, 74, 137
  (*see also* neo-Paretian criterion)
parliament, 15–16, 67, 70–1, 79, 82–4,
    94–5, 103–4, 106, 113, 115, 131,
    134
  and administration, 131
  (*see also* democracy, politicians,
    representation)
participation
  and decision-making costs, 77–8
  and economic welfare, 50–3, 117 (*see*
    also apathy)
  political, 50–3, 77–8, 95–7, 99–100
party cadres, 112–13
paternalism, 7, 103, 117–18, 119, 126,
    134, 151
pay-off matrix, 49, 66
platform, 104–8, 112, 114, 116
point voting, 90–2
polarisation, 107–11
policy
  analysis, 132, 141
  demand for, 32–3, 94–9
  optimum, 98, 108, 112
  outcome of a political system, 15
  polarisation, 107–8
  stand, *see* platform
  supply of, 103, 105, 107–8
political
  behaviour, 87, 96, 99–100, 103–13,
    116
  centre, 79, 99, 106, 116
  culture, 15, 81–2, 103, 151
  economy, 5–6, 13
  participation, *see* participation
  parties, 4, 71, 83, 88, 94–7, 104–6,
    117
  power, *see* power
  process, 7, 15–17, 151–2
  process as production stages, 34,
    144–9, 150
  resources, 95–6, 112
  space, 97–9, 100–2, 107–8, 114
  system, 14–16, 145
  (*see also* information)
politicians, 1, 4, 35–6, 37–9, 67–8, 72,
    94–7, 103–4, 110, 112, 115, 117,

119–21, 125, 127–34, 137–9, 141–2, 144–5, 149, 150, 151
politics, definition of, 4
power
  of bureaucrats, 121–7, 141, 153
  centralisation of, 1, 9–10
  definition of, 9
  economic, 9, 117, 121–2, 153
  equality of, 9, 44, 47, 68, 150–1, 153
  in negotiations, 44, 47, 74, 121–2
  political, 15, 112, 117, 118, 131, 145, 148, 151
  (*see also* monopoly, oligopoly)
preference, ordering of, 20–1, 34, 66, 80–2, 112
pressure groups, 17, 41, 50–3, 87, 96, 113
prisoners' dilemma
  applied to foreign policy, 62–4
  applied to participation, 51
  applied to social goods, 55, 56, 146
  applied to wage information, 65–8
  and coercion, 57, 58, 61, 62, 67
  description of, 48–50
  escape from, 58–61, 63–4, 70
  supergame, 60–1
private goods, 32, 38–9
profit maximisation, 43, 134–7
public finance, theory of, 4, 7, 30, 95
public sector
  growth of, 1–2, 124, 149–53
  optimum size of, 38–40, 149–53
  organisation of, 8, 11

ratio scale, *see* measuring scale
rationality
  definition of, 18–23
  individual and collective, 50
  objective, 22–3, 50
  subjective, 22–3, 42, 97
  (*see also* consistency, information, maximisation, monism, optimum)
referendum democracy
  behaviour of, 77–82, 85–90, 146–8
  definition of, 16, 73, 144
  and economic welfare, 85–93, 146–8, 152
  (*see also* majority decision)
representation
  as a stage of the political process, 16, 94, 144–5, 147–8, 152
representative democracy
  behaviour of, 99–100, 104–8, 147–8

definition of, 16, 94–5, 144
  and economic welfare, 113–20, 147–8, 152
resources, political, 96, 112
responsible behaviour, 58–61

sanctions, 9, 57, 61, 66–7, 70, 121–2, 137, 148, 151
  collective, 70
scarcity, 2–4, 8, 37, 122
self-interest, 42–3, 58–61, 69, 103, 117, 119, 124–5, 138
self-management
  by civil servants, 137–43, 147, 149
  by labour, 139–41, 142–3
selfrating scale, 25, 100–1 (*see also* measuring scale)
simulation
  of negotiations, 64
  of voting behaviour, 101–2
single peakedness, 80–2, 151
social contract, 45, 64
social goods
  characteristics of, 26–8
  definition of, 26
  demand for, 15, 32–4, 127
  economic welfare optimum for, 39–40
  and external effects, 27–8, 58–9
  non-economic, 29
  price of, 33, 95
  pure and impure, 28
  supply of, 103–13, 127–30, 149
  theory of, 6, 149–53
  (*see also* public sector)
social welfare, *see* economic welfare, well being
sociology, 4–5, 13–14, 43, 51, 58, 77, 101–102, 119, 121
span of control, 122–4
stimuli, selective, 57, 58, 64, 146
strategic behaviour, 48, 75, 92–3, 118
structure, *see* centralisation, concentration
symmetry of policy preferences, 98–9, 101, 108, 112

technical efficiency, *see* efficiency
technostructure, 126
totalitarian myth, 121
trade unions, 16, 53–5, 64
transitivity
  Arrow's conditions for, 79–80
  Black's conditions for, 80–1

transitivity—*Contd.*
  definition of, 20
  Sen's conditions for, 81, 148, 151
  (*see also* Arrow paradox,
    consistency)
twoparty system, 107–10, 114–16, 132,
  147, 148, 153

unanimity, 11, 73–4, 115
unimodality, 98–9, 108
UNO, 41, 62–3
unreliability, 106–7, 114
utility
  and altruism, 59
  and class interest, 42–4
  definition of, 19
  as a goal, 18–19
  interpersonal comparison of, 33–5
  interpersonal evaluation of, 34, 91,
    94
  and majority, 73–8
  measurement of, 23–5
  and participation, 51, 96
  and social goods, 30–2
  and voting behaviour, 99–100
utility functions, 108, 112, 114 (*see also*
  objective functions)

value judgments, 34, 37, 71, 74, 94,
  137, 153
value-restrictedness, 81–2, 84, 151

vote trading, *see* logrolling
votes, competition for, 13, 103,
  117–18, 150–1
voting
  behaviour, 99–102
  as active participation, 95–6, 99–100
  systems, 90–3

wage policy, 72 (*see also* democratic
    acceptance of coercion, income
    distribution)
wealth, 25, 101
  definition of, 19
welfare economics
  Bergsonian, 35–6
  definition of, 8
  elements of, 8
  and income distribution, 28, 35, 37,
    64–8, 70–2, 137
  and institutions, 8–9
  Paretian, 24, 36–8
  Pigovian, 24, 35
  as a positive science, 36–7, 71–2, 74,
    137, 153
  (*see also* economic welfare, Pareto
    criterion)
welfare function, economic, 35–6
well-being, 8, 19, 37, 116
workers' council, 116, 139–41, 142–3

zero-sum game, *see* games

Index of names

Abrahamsson, B. 154
Albrow, M. 13, 154
Alker, H. R. 154
Allan, Ch. M. 154
Ames, E. 121, 123, 126, 154
Aristotle, 12
Arrow, K. J. 5, 28, 78–81, 85, 90–2, 145, 146, 154, 160–2
Attali, J. 7, 154

Bacharach, M. 25, 154
Bahrdt, H. P. 154
Balachey, E. L. 18, 158
Barone, E. 8
Barry, B. M. 97, 154
Bartlett, R. 154
Baumol, W. J. 5, 8, 154
Bélanger, G. 158
Bentham, J. 43
Berg, E. L. 118, 154
Bergson, A. 35, 154
Bergstrom, Th. C 154
Bernholz, P. 154
Bish, R. L. 76, 154
Black, D. 78, 80, 81, 83, 90, 154
Blau, P. M. 14, 124, 154
Blydenburgh, J. C. 82, 154
Bohm, P. 154
Bolingbroke, H. S.-J. 115
Borcherding, Th. E. 154, 159
Bowen, H. R. 154
Brams, S. J. 155
Braybrooke, D. 11, 155
Breton, A. 53, 96, 126, 131, 132, 155
Buchanan, J. M. 5, 27, 44–7, 75–7, 83, 94, 152, 153, 155
Budge, I, 159
Burgess, Ph. M. 64, 155
Burkhead, J. 155

Callaghan, J. 64
Campbell, A. 97, 155

Carlyle, T. 108
Carson, R. B. 155
Carson, R. L. 155
Cartter, A. M. 158
Chammah, A. M. 160
Coleridge, S. T. 97
Cramer, J. S. 157
Crozier, M. 13, 124, 155
Crutchfield, S. 18, 158
Curry, R. L. 162
Cyert, R. M. 22, 155

Daalder, H. 52, 142, 155
Dahl, R. A. 12, 86, 93, 112, 119, 120, 133, 142, 155
Davis, O. A. 98, 99, 155
De Beus, J. W. 155
De Borda, J.-C. 90–3, 155
De Condorcet, M. J. A. N. Marquis, 78, 158
De Galan, C. 64, 65, 68, 72, 152, 162
De Maistre, J. 97
De Meester, T. H. 88
De Swaan, A. 106, 155
De Toqueville, A. 12, 13, 119, 155
De Wolff, P. 157
Den Uyl, J. M. 35, 64
Dobb, M. 155
Dodgson, C. L. 78
Dole, M. 155
Downs, A. 5, 14, 97–9,103, 104, 106, 114, 115, 118, 125, 133, 152, 156
Drees, W. 134, 152, 156
Dror, Y. 50, 156

Easton, D. 4, 14, 15, 156
Ellemers, J. E. 9, 156
Ellman, M. J. 65, 156
Engels, F. 42, 156, 158
Etzioni, A. 14
Eucken, W. 10, 11, 156

172   *Index of names*

Faludi, A. 138, 156
Farquharson, R. 82, 156
Frey, B. S. 5, 7, 117, 156
Frohlich, N. 7, 156

Gäfgen, G. 156
Gaile, C. 160
Galbraith, J. K. 121, 126, 132, 133, 152, 156
Gandhi, V. P. 156
Gawthrop, L. C. 163
Godelier, M. 156
Goldwater, B. 113
Goodman, R. P. 154
Gossen, H. H. 30, 31
Gouldner, A. 124
Graicunas, A. V. 122, 123
Grondsma, T. 15, 157
Guggenberger, B. 157

Hamilton, A. 93
Han Fei Tzu 62
Hart, K. D. 161
Hayek, F. A. 11, 157
Head, J. G. 26, 28, 157
Heertje, A. 157
Hegel, G. F. W. 43, 97
Hennipman, P. xi, 19, 22, 27, 34, 37, 74, 157
Herbst, Ph. G. 157
Hicks, J. R. 37, 139
Hinich, M. J. 98–100, 103–5, 155, 157
Hirsch, F. 59, 65, 157
Hirschman, A. O. 112, 113, 115, 157
Hobbes, T. 62, 152, 159
Hoogerwerf, A. 103, 157
Houghton, D. 159
Hotelling, H. 104, 108, 112, 157
Howard, N. 157
Hume, D. 62

In't Veld, R. J. 157
Irwin, G. A. 100, 157

Jefferson, T. 12, 13
Johansen, L. 44, 47, 157

Kafoglis, M. Z. 57, 157
Kaldor, N. 37
Kapteyn, A. 157, 162
Key, V. O. 97, 100, 157
Keynes, J. M. 78
King, A. G. 158
Kirschen, E. S. 41, 157

Klaassen, L. H. 161
Klant, J. J. 20, 157
Klaver, J. A. M. 6, 158
Kogan, M. 159
Koo, A. Y. C. 21
Kornai, J. 21, 158
Körner, S. 161
Krech, D. 18, 158
Kuypers, G. 158

Lammers, C. J. 51, 62, 158
Lange, O. 8, 158, 161
Leibenstein, H. 158
Lijphart, A. 82, 158
Lincoln, A. 12, 13
Lindahl, E. 44, 47, 48, 52, 144, 158
Lindblom, Ch. E. 20, 21, 25, 118, 158
Little, I. M. D. 25, 158
Loasby, B. J. 158
Locke, J. 12
Luce, R. D. 48, 158

McGovern, G. 113
McGuire, C. B. 158, 161
McKenzie, R. B. 158
Madison, J. 12, 93
Mannheim, K. 7, 153, 158
March, J. G. 22, 155
Marschak, J. 158
Marshall, A. 24, 31, 158
Marshall, F. M. 158
Marx, K. 42, 43, 52, 56, 158
May, K. O. M. 20
Mayston, D. J. 158
Mazzola, U. 7
Meade, J. E. 140, 158
Meij, J. L. 122
Meissner, W. 156
Merkies, A. H. Q. M. 35, 158
Merton, R. 124
Mestmäcker, E. J. 156
Michels, R. 14, 77, 158, 162
Migué, J. L. 158
Mill, J. S. 13, 14, 158
Millward, R. 26, 27, 158
Miner, J. 155
Mishan, E. J. 31, 158
Mitchell, W. C. 4, 159
Mitnick, B. M. 159
Montias, J. M. 159
Morgenstern, O. 24, 25, 162
Moss, L. S. 152, 159
Mouzelis, N. P. 124
Mueller, D. C. 5, 7, 90, 159

Musgrave, P. B. 3, 26, 38, 159
Musgrave, R. A. 3, 5, 26, 30, 38, 53, 73, 158, 159, 163
Myrdal, G. 159

Nath, S. K. 36, 159
Niemi, R. G. 91–3, 159
Niskanen, W. A. 5, 121, 122, 126–32, 134, 135, 149, 152, 155, 159, 161
Noordzij, G. P. 159
Nove, A. 121, 124, 125, 135, 159

O'Connor, J. 159
Olson, M. 5, 42, 43, 51–3, 56–8, 62–4, 68, 100, 159
Oppenheimer, J. A. 7, 156
Ordeshook, P. C. 7, 20, 23, 28, 34, 79, 81, 82, 92, 98–100, 103–5, 107, 108, 110, 114, 115, 155, 157, 159, 160
Orzechowski, W. 132, 137, 159
Ostrom, V. 4, 121, 159

Paelinck, J. H. P. 158
Page, A. N. 159
Palmer, M. 160
Pareto, V. 4, 8, 24, 35–8, 59, 61, 68, 74, 89, 113, 137, 157, 160
Parkinson, C. N. 124
Parsons, T. 14
Peacock, A. T. 30, 36, 53, 73, 79, 158–60, 163
Pen J. 79, 80, 122, 160
Phelps, E. S. 156
Philpotts, G. C. 159
Pigou, A. C. 4, 24, 35, 160
Plato 38, 114
Price, C. M. 160
Pryor, F. L. 1, 61, 160

Rabushka, A. 161
Radner, R. 158, 161
Raiffa, H. 48, 158
Rapoport, A. 160
Rheinstein, M. 18, 160
Ridley, N. 159
Riker, W. H. 5, 7, 20, 23, 28, 34, 79, 81, 82, 91–3, 98–100, 103, 104, 107, 108, 112, 114, 115, 117, 159, 160
Robbins, L. 2, 6, 9, 18, 160
Robertson, D. 109–11, 160
Robinson, J. A. 64, 155
Röpke, W. 11, 160
Ross, S. A. 160

Rothenberg, J. 25, 34, 160
Rothschild, K. W. 160
Rousseau, J.-J. 12
Rowley, Ch. K. 36, 79, 157, 160
Russet, B. M. 160

Sahni, B. S. 160
Salamon, L. M. 96, 160
Samuelson, P. A. 30, 32, 38, 160
Sauermann, H. 156
Sax, E. 7, 30
Scherer, F. M. 135, 160
Schmidt, L. R. 160
Schmidt, O. 56, 160
Schneider, F. 156
Schumacher, E. F. 58, 160
Schumpeter, J. A. 13, 16, 117, 150, 161
Scitovsky, T. 26, 28, 38, 135, 139, 154, 160, 161
Scott, H. A. 14, 161
Selznick, P. 124
Sen, A. K. 59, 60, 69, 81, 161
Senior, I. 159
Shaffer, W. R. 101, 102, 161
Shepherd, W. G. 161
Shepsle, K. A. 161
Shubik, M. 114, 161
Siccama, J. G. 6, 137, 142, 158, 161
Siegfried, J. J. 96, 160
Simon, H. Λ. 14, 21, 22, 161
Smith, A. 3
Smith, J. 156
Sproule-Jones, M. 161
Stapel, J. 101
Stern, L. 160
Sterne, R. S. 161
Stevers, Th. A. 161
Stigler, G. J. 97, 161
Sweezy, P. M. 161

Taylor, F. M. 158
Taylor, M. 5, 58, 60–2, 152, 161
Thoben, H. A. A. M. 63, 64, 161
Thomassen, J. 100, 157
Thompson, E. A. 131, 132, 161
Tinbergen, J. xi, 8, 26, 64, 65, 68, 72, 114, 152, 161, 162
Tollison, R. T. 5, 155
Tucker, A. W. 48
Tufte, E. R. 155
Tullock, G. 5, 75–7, 83, 94, 124, 128, 139, 152, 155, 158, 162

Van der Linden, C. 89

Van der Veen, R. J. 56, 160
Van Doorn, J. J. A. 77, 162
Van Praag, B. M. S. 25, 162
Van Schendelen, M. 159, 162
Van Thijn, E. 115, 162
Vanek, J. 139–42, 159, 162
Veblen, T. 43, 162
Von Mises, L. 14, 162
Von Neumann, J. 24, 25, 162

Wade, L. L. 162
Wagner, A. 4, 156
Wagner, R. E. 155
Waldo, D. 4, 163
Walpole, R. 115
Walras, L. 4
Weber, M. 9, 13, 14, 18, 121, 143, 149, 163

Weitenberg, J. 158
Wemelsfelder, J. 142, 163
Wicksell, K. 7, 30, 43, 53, 56, 57, 62, 64, 73, 75, 163
Wilensky, H. L. 61, 163
Wiles, P. J. D. 6, 125, 163
Williamson, O. E. 121, 126, 127, 131, 132, 134, 163
Wilson, H. 64
Wilson, W. 121, 163
Winch, D. M. 28, 163
Wintrobe, R. 126, 131, 132, 155
Wittman, D. A. 118, 163
Wright Mills, C. 43, 163

Young, O. R. 156

Zeckhauser, R. 62, 63, 159